THE FUNCTION OF ASSESSMENT WITHIN PSYCHOLOGICAL THERAPIES

THE FUNCTION OF ASSESSMENT WITHIN PSYCHOLOGICAL THERAPIES

A PSYCHODYNAMIC VIEW

Kamran Ghaffari
Luigi Caparrotta

KARNAC

LONDON   NEW YORK

First published in 2004 by
H. Karnac (Books) Ltd.
6 Pembroke Buildings, London NW10 6RE

British Library Cataloguing in Publication Data

A C.I.P. for this book is available from the British Library

ISBN 1 85575 954 3

Edited, designed and produced by The Studio Publishing Services Ltd, Exeter EX4 8JN

Printed in Great Britain

10 9 8 7 6 5 4 3 2 1

www.karnacbooks.com

CONTENTS

To our wives, Farnaz and Sara

ACKNOWLEDGEMENTS

This book is the result of many years of training and clinical experience and we are indebted to our analysts, supervisors, teachers, colleagues, friends and, most of all, our patients. Although we have endeavoured to be as objective as possible, we cannot deny the impact of our personal and cultural background.

We are particularly grateful to Professor Phil Richardson for his warm encouragement and suggestions, to Amaryllis Holland for her diplomatic and brilliant editing skills, to Dr Sheilagh Davies for taking the time to read our first draft, and for their valuable comments.

Most of all we would like to thank our wives, Farnaz and Sara, who tolerated our moods and sporadic absences while supporting our endeavour.

PREFACE

The past few decades have borne witness to a proliferation of psychotherapeutic approaches. Over 450 variants of psychological therapy have been identified (Richardson, 1997), although most represent subclasses of a smaller number of major orientations. Each variant is based on different theoretical models, has different standards of training, different standards of practice, and different accrediting bodies and professional organizations. However, all have the common aim of alleviating psychological suffering.

Various theoretical models have placed different emphasis and importance on the role of assessment. We strongly believe that this first encounter not only has a prime and unique position in any form of psychological therapy, but often paves the way and sets the scene for any therapeutic process to develop.

The increased demand for psychological therapy, the formal recognition of its effectiveness and its role in the treatment of a wide variety of mental health problems, including severe and enduring illness, have rendered careful, accurate assessment crucial.

However, there is very little formal training in assessing patients for suitability for psychological therapy (Cooper & Alfillé, 1998).

A number of attempts have been made to standardize the assessment process, but their impact on everyday clinical practice is limited.

The aim of this book is to attempt to bridge this gap by providing guidelines for assessment for psychological therapy, informed by the authors' clinical practice, the Department of Health recommendations, and the available evidence. A further aim is to bring together different aspects of the assessment process, which can be found scattered in a number of edited specialist books and journals.

Our purpose has been to keep the book as simple as possible so that it may be easily accessible to beginners as well as as providing an initial structure and overview for more experienced practitioners. We hope, therefore, that this work may serve as a useful guide for referrers, trainees, and therapists practising in a variety of psychotherapeutic settings, including those in the National Health Service and in private practice, and that it will begin to foster further debate in this field.

Clinical vignettes and case examples have been used throughout the book in order to illustrate and simplify the various stages of the complex process of assessment. Patients' anonymity has been respected and personal details have been altered as far as possible to preserve confidentiality.

FOREWORD

While manuals of psychotherapy abound, there is a surprising shortage of high quality texts devoted to the techniques and processes of assessment for psychotherapy. There are several possible reasons for this.

The first arises from the frequent conflation of clinical assessment with diagnosis. In conventional medical circles, recognition of the importance of accurate diagnostic assessment is axiomatic. Without knowing what we are dealing with how can we possibly treat it? In psychiatry, the relationships between diagnosis and treatment, as between diagnosis and prognosis, are less convincingly established than in many branches of medicine. If a specific diagnosis does not imply a specific treatment and if an individual treatment method can be shown to be helpful for a diversity of different conditions (or diagnoses)—as would appear to be the case where psychotherapy is concerned—then the importance of diagnostic assessment will be diminished, since it will be less relevant to any eventual course of therapeutic action.

Moreover, many lay and non-medical psychotherapists consider that conducting a diagnostic assessment implies the endorsement of a medical perspective on human distress and hence fail to acknowledge the importance of an individualized psychological perspective on the person in need. Therapy is no longer equated with "treatment" in the medical sense, and the person seeking therapy is no longer considered a "patient". Early theoretical, political, and ideological debates in this area (as embodied in the works of Szasz, Laing and others) have more recently largely been superseded by a perspective deriving from an increased emphasis on the public accountability of all public sector professionals, including those who offer services in the domain of mental health. Patients are increasingly viewed as users or consumers of services who have a right to involvement in decisions concerning their care and/or treatment—hence, no longer to be seen as the passive recipients of the latter. This places the individual patient/service user at the centre of the healthcare enterprise and again reduces the diagnosis to only one of a number of factors that might determine the course of treatment/intervention.

In addition, the ascendancy of non-medical mental health professionals (clinical psychologists, lay psychotherapists) in recent years has given increasing weight to the eschewal of conventional psychiatric diagnostic practice in mental health care provision. While partly driven by professional tribalism, the challenge to illness-related conceptions of mental health—embodied in a psychosocial view of mental disorder—has done much to broaden the scope of psychological treatment approaches as well as their accessibility.

A counter-thrust to this trend has been the development of a certain form of healthcare practice which is described as "evidence-based". Evidence-based practice (EBP) refers to a way of working which involves "integrating individual, clinical expertise with the best available external clinical evidence from systematic research" (Sackett et al., 1996). Such an approach implies the need to characterize and classify that evidence and, despite much debate on the most appropriate way to do this where psychotherapy is concerned (cf. Richardson, 2001), the clearest consensus would seem to support the use of diagnostic categories for this purpose (Roth & Fonagy, 1996). If the evidence for the treatments we offer is sorted according to the "conditions" for which those treatments are designed, then an evidence-based approach to healthcare requires accurate identification of the condition to be treated. Sadly for the proponents of this approach, at least where psychotherapy is concerned, the available empirical evidence offers little reassurance. A wealth of factors—altogether independent of the diagnostic status of the patient—has been shown to have a powerful influence on therapeutic outcome. Foremost among these are the theoretical allegiance of the researchers studying the therapy concerned, and the quality of the relationship between the therapist and the patient—regardless of the style of therapy under investigation (cf. Orlinsky *et al.*, 2004).

It is much to be appreciated that the authors of the present volume do not slip into an overly comfortable identification with the contemporary party line of diagnostically-driven evidence-based practice. Assessment remains necessary, of course, to the extent that clarity about the task facing the psychotherapist is essential. Holding firm to a psychological, and essentially psychodynamic, perspective on human distress, their starting point for the evaluation of the psychotherapeutic needs of the individual presenting to any mental health service, is that individual's unique constellation of experiences—a constellation that cannot be summarized in the form of an *ICD-10* or *DSM-IV* diagnosis. For Ghaffari and Caparrotta, the process of assessment implies identifying the therapeutic needs of the individual in relation to his or her own personal psychology, history and circumstances. Assessment is no longer conceived as a process of accurate identification of "what is wrong with the patient"—in a global diagnostic sense; rather it is seen as being about exploring and understanding the developmental and therapeutic tasks facing an individual in need.

Both authors are psychiatrists, psychoanalysts, and psychotherapists with extensive clinical and training experience in the National Health Service as well as in the private sector. They are to be congratulated for drawing on this wealth of experience to produce a book of rare quality in an area of accomplishment which has so far evaded some of the best writers in the field. Of particular note is their extensive use of clinical material to bring to life their insights—thereby providing the most compelling illustration of the role of clinical judgement in evidence-based practice.

This book will be enormously helpful to psychiatry, clinical psychology, psychotherapy, social work, and mental health nursing trainees who face the daunting task of conducting their first psychodynamic assessments. It offers not only solid theoretical foundations for the tasks of psychotherapy assessment but also good, clear, practical guidance for every stage of the assessment process. Many experienced clinicians will also find it useful to be reminded about why they are doing what they are doing—especially when they are doing it well!

Phil Richardson
Professor of Clinical Psychology, Tavistock Clinic

REFERENCES

Laing, R. A. (1967). *The Politics of Experience*. New York: Pantheon.
Orlinsky, D., Rønnested, M., & Willutzki, U. (2004). Fifty years of psychotherapy process outcome research: continuity and change. In: *Bergin and Garfield's Handbook of Psychotherapy and Behavior Change* (5th edn) (pp. 307–389). New York: John Wiley and Sons.
Richardson, P. (2001). Evidence-based practice and the psychodynamic psychotherapies. In: C. Mace, S. Moorey, & B. Roberts (Eds.), *Evidence in the Psychological Therapies* (pp. 157–173). London: Routledge.
Roth, A., & Fonagy, P., (1996). *What Works for Whom? A Critical Review of Psychotherapy Research*. New York: Guildford Press.
Sackett, D., Rosenberg, W., Gray, J., Haynes, R., & Richardson, W. (1996). Evidence-based medicine: what it is and what it is not (Editorial). *British Medical Journal*, 312: 71–72.
Szasz, T. S. (1970). *The Manufacture of Madness*. New York: Dell.

Introduction

"Why should anyone be afraid of change?"

Marcus Aurelius

National Health Service model and expectations

In so far as the new millennium is the product of the old in that contemporary conditions are shaped by the past, the issue of "modernizing" healthcare has a long history marked by constantly shifting expectations entertained by the public and professionals alike.

Founded in 1948, the National Health Service (NHS), in spite of its imperfections, was considered one of the jewels in the British crown. It was envied to such a degree that it was adopted as a model for numerous health services around the world.

The NHS advanced steadily for a number of years, not only because of the high quality service it provided, but also as a result of an impressive amount of goodwill on behalf of its staff. However, it rapidly became evident that, in order to function effectively and efficiently, it would be imperative that the NHS kept abreast of the rapidly changing face of society's expectations (Sennett, 1998).

Inevitably, increases in life expectancy, the rapid expansion of medical knowledge within the public domain, and advances in communication and technology have resulted in high expectations on the part of patients and policymakers alike. The dictum "infinite demand and finite resources" (Bhugra & Burns, 1995) has remained appropriate throughout the chequered history of the NHS. Furthermore, some of us would even maintain that recent times have borne witness to a growing pressure on the NHS to "cure" or, at the very least, manage the ills of modern society.

Successive governments have responded with extravagant promises and high targets for service delivery, with little regard for already stretched health resources. Repeatedly, the onus has been placed firmly on the shoulders of the overburdened health profes- sionals, whose frequent dissatisfaction is clearly linked to overwork and lack of support. Such an unfortunate combination has been shown to be the principal reason for low morale and early retire- ment (Smith, 2001).

The growth of consumerism and the increasing demand for public accountability of professionals have been accompanied by a parallel change in the quality of patient–doctor relationships and an atmosphere of blame has come to prevail, fostered by "stories of errors outnumbering tales of triumph" (Smith, ibid.). The result has been a shaky trust in a medical profession no longer regarded as the sole repository of medical scientific knowledge. Furthermore, developments such as patients' self-determination and the right to be informed have led people to begin to question the validity and efficacy of a number of medical practices and procedures.

The commendable introduction to the Patients' Charter, along with more stringent criteria for "evidence-based medicine" (some- times difficult to reconcile with the other fundamental tenet of "patient choice"), "quality control" and "clinical governance", together constitute an attempt to address at least some of these issues. Unfortunately, however, they have also paved the way to a fundamental and dangerous combination of unrealistic, even omnipotent, expectations on the part of the patient as well as the doctor, with each expecting what the other is unable to deliver. This gap between expectations and reality was aptly commented upon

(Editor's choice, *British Medical Journal*, 2000), leading to the conclusion that "We need simultaneously to improve reality and reduce expectations".

Mental health and the role of psychological therapies

Continual advances in terms of scientific knowledge and our ability to detect illness, the desire for a better quality of life, the government's drive for early detection, and the public demand for better protection from dangerous behaviour have even stronger implications for the provision of mental health services.

Even though psychotherapy is recognized as a driving force within mental health services, providing "a meaning for the patient's suffering and a source of hope" (Knud, 1999) and contributing substantially within the general framework of a comprehensive hospital and community mental health care, it has remained barely visible to date (Garelick, 1998). Only recently have efforts been made formally to include "psychological therapies" as part of integral planning for mental health care (Holmes, 2002).

Nevertheless, the demand for psychotherapy in primary and secondary care has increased steadily, revealing even more clearly a lack of provision and an unequal distribution of services. A comprehensive review of the NHS psychotherapy services in England (Parry & Richardson, 1996), commissioned by the Department of Health (DoH), began to investigate and address some of these issues. The authors examined the generic use of the term "psychotherapy", along with training, provision, and integration of psychotherapy services and identified the confusion that has resulted from the use of the generic term "psychotherapy" in the past. They attempted to define and clarify the delivery of psychotherapy and recommended that the full range of major psychotherapies should be subsumed under the term "psychological therapies". This embraces most forms of psychotherapy available in the NHS, such as psychoanalytic (focal psychodynamic and psychoanalytic), cognitive-behavioural, systemic, eclectic, and integrative interventions for adult patients.

In examining the delivery of psychological therapies, three distinctive elements of psychotherapeutic work were identified:

(1) Type A (integral)—general psychotherapeutic skills provided by any mental health worker within a multidisciplinary care package.

(2) Type B (generic)—a complete ("stand-alone") psychological treatment intervention informed by a range of different models, tailored to individual goals—including generic counselling.

(3) Type C (formal)—a complete ("stand-alone") and clearly delineated psychotherapeutic intervention based on a clear theoretical framework with implications for the use of different treatment interventions to achieve different aims.

Any of these modalities may be offered on individual, group, couple, and family bases.

Furthermore, the review emphasized the need to integrate services that provide psychological therapies, to formalize training and develop quality standards, including assessment guidelines, in order to deliver a more coordinated, safe, cost-effective, and user-friendly service to all groups of mentally ill patients.

We applaud this review and believe that in time it will lead not only to more flexibility in deciding the appropriate type of intervention, but also to the possibility of matching the patient's difficulties to a specific therapeutic model and, where possible, to a suitable therapist.

For the purpose of this book, we broadly define psychological therapy as any form of psychological treatment that aims to produce a desired change in emotions, cognition and behaviour in the context of a relationship between a patient or group of patients and a trained professional.

The role of assessment within psychological therapies

It is within this context that we consider it timely to examine in detail an important component of our specialist daily work: *the function of assessment in psychological therapies with particular reference to psychodynamic assessment.* We think that this procedure represents an interesting and informative micro-process within the complex web of interaction between patient–doctor and society and that the examination thereof may give rise to further discussion of some of the aforementioned conflicts.

By focusing on assessment, we shall inevitably encounter some of the expectations developing as a result of these interactions and learn from them. In addition, this investigation represents an attempt to shed some light on the reality-based issues faced when working within the NHS, including an awareness of both our limited resources and our own limitations, as well as an acknowledgement of the realities and expectations of our patients.

First we shall concentrate on the definition of assessment, the role of the assessor, and the process of referral, before moving on to the assessment phase proper and eventual therapeutic allocation. We acknowledge that the use of these artificial divisions may inhibit our depiction of the fluidity of the whole process, but we felt it necessary for the sake of clarity. However, we have attempted to make pertinent links, where appropriate, between the various sections, in order to give a more holistic picture of the entire process.

The following chapters are based primarily on many years of experience in our respective psychological therapy services in the context of comprehensive NHS mental health service provision and private psychoanalytic practice, and therefore may not be representative of all psychological therapies in their diversity (Parry & Richardson, 1996).

We are aware that our medical, psychiatric, and psychoanalytic perspectives will be apparent throughout this volume. We firmly believe that experience in a general psychiatric setting and within a multidisciplinary context is fundamental to a sensitive diagnostic assessment, which we consider to be necessary for an appropriate choice of treatment.

CHAPTER ONE

Definition of assessment

F irst interview, consultation, diagnostic evaluation, therapeutic encounter, assessment interview, and clinical interview are some of the terms employed to describe the process of assessment.

Before defining and examining the various components of the assessment procedure, it may be informative to examine the etymology of the word "assessment". The derivation of "assessment" comprises both the Latin *ad-sedere* (*to sit at or by*) and the French *assise* (*to size*) representing a standard of conduct, *an extent*, a magnitude, etc. (Partridge, 1966). Viewed within this context, assessment seems to have very definite legal connotations that could be associated with an intrusive, judgemental attitude.

Hence assessment, in a clinical setting, can be defined simply as a process of *sitting* together and spending time with a professional to establish the nature and the *extent* of the presenting problem in the context of one's own narrative at a particular stage of one's own life. This interaction should afford the patient an opportunity for self-exploration with another person in a safe, non-judgemental atmosphere.

In practice, however, such a process requires professional skill and presents numerous challenges. Moreover, it is well recognized that the assessment of a patient for psychotherapy is a very complex procedure. Coltart (1986), in her seminal article on assessment, makes it very clear that the clinical interview exploits a combination of diagnostic efforts and skilful interaction to search for the subtle nuances which should lead to "a psychotherapy prescription". Even the best-conducted psychotherapy consultation cannot escape the delicate, intricate, and subtle interaction that is often a source of apprehension for both the assessor and the interviewee. Indeed, this interaction may be the source of the most valuable information (Davies, 2003).

Definition and function of the assessor

The New Oxford Dictionary defines "assessor" as *"a person, who is knowledgeable in a particular field and is called upon for advice"*. When applied to psychological therapies this definition requires expansion. In 1979, Malan cogently pointed out that

> the preliminary enquiry can only be carried out effectively by someone [*assessor*] well grounded in theoretical knowledge . . . as well as experienced in the different possible kinds of intervention and the consequences of applying them in many different situations.

Milton (1997) stresses that the definition of the assessor within psychological therapies is not only beset by questions regarding training, experience, and theoretical positions, but also by those relating to individual style.

Ideally, the assessor conducting the initial assessment should be a senior clinician, highly trained, familiar with local facilities, and informed by research. The recent document from the NHS Executive (2000) stresses the importance of assessments being conducted by widely experienced psychological therapists and sets out minimum requirements for training. These are :

> (i) a core professional training in mental health and at least 6 months experience of working therapeutically with the severe and enduring mentally ill; (ii) a foundation training (minimum 30 hours incorporating theoretical and clinical seminars for each

model) in a broad range (>3) of major psychological therapies with "practitioner" status (minimum 2 year training) in at least one.

We agree with the NHS Executive's recommendation of minimum requirements for training, but believe that for the purpose of assessment a longer and more intensive training is to be highly recommended (minimum four years).

The attitude of the assessor and the style in which the diagnostic interview is conducted are vital components of the assessment process and its outcome. We believe, therefore, that the diagnostician should attempt to create a safe space for the patient to explore his/her difficulties by adopting a warm, flexible stance and by working as an active and intuitive participant. Furthermore, the assessor should actively engage the patient with empathy, flexibility, elicit his/her collaboration, convey that he/she is valued and acknowledge his/her uniqueness and point of view (Gabbard, 2000). The initial assessment is a joint venture and should be "patient-centred" rather than "pass or fail" interview to fit in with the assessor's view (Davies, 2003). As illustrated below, it is not uncommon for some assessing clinicians to adopt a detached, cold, and even silent posture.

> After 10 minutes of silence, Mr A asked the assessor, tongue-in-cheek, whether they were waiting for the tea to arrive, as it was teatime. The assessor interpreted this statement by telling the patient that he was obviously very hungry to be fed by him. Mr. A, renowned for his humour, responded by asking the assessor whether they were waiting for biscuits to arrive with their tea. After a few more minutes of silence, Mr A eventually walked out saying that he would rather prefer the warmth of the canteen.

As Coltart (1988) emphasizes, this stance is very often adopted by assessors, based on the unfortunate assumption that such a stance might encourage the expression of patients' anxieties, thereby facilitating access to deeper unconscious conflicts. Kohut (1996), in his 1975 lecture, ventures beyond this to point out that the artificial absence of an empathic response is not only depriving but clearly unhelpful. He claims that it is a mistake to interpret the consequent rage generated in the patient as an expression of ". . . his true self coming out"! In our experience, an unresponsive and detached posture can increase the patient's already heightened anxieties about exposure, which can be counterproductive and possibly lead to premature foreclosure. Furthermore, the assessor may form an image of the patient that is partial, if not distorted (Coltart, 1988; Diatkine, 1968; Limentani, 1972). Similarly, the patient may be left with a flawed impression of how this type of first encounter could be useful, let alone lead to a therapeutic endeavour.

While excessive detachment on the part of the assessor can be unhelpful, it is equally important that we avoid either inviting the patient to like us (to satisfy our own narcissistic needs), or making it so comfortable that the assessment becomes little more than a cosy chat with a friend. Within this context, the need to respect the patient cannot be emphasized enough.

Clinical experience, including training, and, to some extent, the theoretical allegiances and cultural background of the assessor, are important contributors to the assessment. Other assessor variables include gender, age, religious beliefs, and socio-economic background.

While some factors are inherent to the assessor, there are also factors that are brought to the assessment by the patient, as well as factors deriving from the interaction between the two.

The following examples serve to illustrate some of these factors.

A patient was offered an appointment for assessment by one of us (KG). On receipt of the appointment letter she rang the secretary declining the consultation because she did not want to see anyone with a foreign name.

Cultural awareness and sensitivity, as part of a broader dimension of individual sensitivity, have become increasingly important in our multicultural society and should therefore be included in any training.

A Muslim woman with depression and anxiety was referred for assessment for psychological therapy. The assessor, unaware of the cultural conventions, tried to shake the patient's hand when introducing himself. This oversight caused the woman to be defensive and unhelpful during the assessment. "If he can not understand my cultural background how can he help?"

While shaking hands may create problems, not shaking hands can just as easily lead to misunderstandings, leaving the patient asking him/herself why the assessor seemed so rude and dismissive.

To disclose one's own inner world to a "stranger" is not an easy accomplishment. Such intimate disclosure is often accompanied by fears of being judged and found out, which may give way to a mixture of dread and anticipation and ultimately hamper the patient's ability to convey freely the extent of his/her difficulties. Milton (2001), for example, emphasizes that a good assessor should be able to gauge the patient's capacity to tolerate intrusion. He/she should not be afraid to ask questions (Busch, 1986), but equally, bombarding patients with too many questions can be disconcerting and lead to uncomfortable recoil. This fear of intrusion can be detected even before meeting the patient.

> A questionnaire was sent to Miss K before her initial assessment. She returned it blank aside from her name and address. She arrived for her appointment with her boyfriend and agreed to be interviewed only if he was also present. She started by saying that she found it very difficult to write anything or even to talk about herself to a total stranger. It took three consultations before she felt relaxed enough to leave the boyfriend sitting in the waiting room and to trust the assessor.

At the opposite end of the spectrum it is not uncommon to encounter an eagerness to talk and express strong emotions during the first interview. The opportunity to talk about oneself in the presence of a "listening ear" is a unique opportunity, which can be perceived not only as liberating but also as satisfying a long-standing need to be taken seriously.

> Mrs B was referred by her general practitioner for panic attacks. When questioned about her difficulties, she started to talk painfully about the past twenty years of her life. At the end of the assessment, she left smiling, thanking the interviewer for being the first person to give her the space and attention she had been longing for.

In conclusion, we would like to emphasize that assessment is an intricate and delicate interplay between two individuals with their own unique life histories. As Anna Freud (1954) points out, it amounts to "two real people of equal adult status and in real relationship to each other" involved in a process of mutual exploration into the known and the unknown, the links, the fears, and the hopes, and the wish both to know and not know. Invariably this new experience will draw on the life experiences, or the lack thereof, of both the interviewee and the assessor. Furthermore, it will always combine the skills, talents, and expertise of the assessor with the attributions and expectations of the patient that define the journey.

CHAPTER TWO

The referral process

Pre-referral stage

We consider it pertinent to highlight this "pre-referral stage", for we believe that it may have an impact on the patient's decision regarding whether or not to attend a psychotherapy consultation.

The referral process evolves from the interaction between patient and referrer. The decision to initiate the referral process may be taken by the referrer, the patient, or both. Experienced referrers tend to discuss the process and merits of "talking therapy" with the patient, which may help them to reach a decision. On the other hand, referrers with a very limited knowledge of psychotherapy may set the process in motion by prescribing "psychotherapy", without giving an adequate explanation of the reasons for this decision or of the benefits the patient may derive from such an intervention. Increasingly, patients tend to request a psychotherapy referral.

Having mutually decided that "talking therapy" would be helpful, the referrer needs to choose the most appropriate setting; e.g. in-house counselling, specialist hospital based services, private referral. For example, in the Primary Care setting, the majority of cases in which problems are mild and stress-related could be dealt with by the in-house counsellor, particularly if the patient prefers not to be referred to a hospital-based specialist service. However, the ability to make such a decision is determined by the availability of properly trained and supervised counsellors within the practice.

Referral source and reasons for referral

Referrals usually come from psychiatrists, general practitioners, Community Mental Health Teams (CMHTs), psychologists, social workers, and other medical or non-medical sources. Broadly speaking, more than half of referrals to our busy specialist psychotherapy out-patient services tend to be made by general psychiatrists, approximately 40% by general practitioners, with the remainder coming from professionals within the service and other sources.

The reasons for referral, upon which we will expand in the next chapter on pre-specialist assessment, include the following:

● for assessment for treatment of choice
● as an adjunct to the overall management
● as an alternative to drug therapy
● poor compliance with medication
● therapeutic stalemate
● when disturbance of personality hinders treatment progress.

However, this list of reasons is not exhaustive and very often patients are referred for a combination of these reasons.

Referral letter

A letter continues to be the most frequent mode of referral. This can be addressed either to a named specialist or to a named service.

The content of referral letters is wide-ranging. It can vary from non-informative statements, such as "please see and treat", to very detailed histories that might include an indication of suitability for psychological therapy and suggestions regarding appropriate psychotherapy types and modalities.

In our opinion a helpful letter should contain, in addition to demographic data, at least the following information:

- presenting problems
- a brief history of the onset
- previous contact with mental health services
- relevant medical history
- reasons for referral
- brief note indicating that patient has been fully informed.

Such information facilitates the preliminary screening and appropriate assessment route. It allows for the gathering of relevant details, when there has been previous known contact with psychiatrists, psychologists, CMHTs, or other services. If need be, relevant discussion with such agencies can be embarked upon. Moreover, this information may provide an initial guide to the most appropriate way for assessing that particular patient.

The following extreme case illustrates our concern regarding non-informative letters:

> A 29-year-old male patient was referred by his GP, who wrote a letter stating simply that the patient was suffering from marked anxiety symptoms. The patient had to wait a number of weeks to be seen. Only at the assessment did the assessor realize that the patient spoke no English.

An informative letter referring a complex case may lead to a discussion, ideally within a multidisciplinary psychological therapies setting. From these discussions a decision can then be reached regarding the selection of the most appropriate assessment procedure, focusing on minimizing disruption for the patient, and thereby reducing the risk of "shunting" patients from one service to another.

Referral route

The referral route selected by the referrer depends on a number of factors:

- availability and ease of access to a specialist service
- referrer's level of acquaintance with the assessing clinicians
- referrer's knowledge and attitude to a specific treatment modality.

The referral route may sometimes be selected on an *ad hoc* basis. In some localities the referrer may be faced with fragmented, uncoordinated, and artificially separated services.

In order to address the problem of unnecessary multiple assessments, the NHS Executive (April, 2000) suggested a single portal of entry as a way of streamlining the referral route and minimizing multiple assessments and "false starts" in treatment.

Occasionally, however, it may be necessary for the patient to be re-assessed by another colleague in order to eliminate unnecessary, at times even deleterious, therapeutic options. After all, psychological intervention, like any other form of treatment, has its indications and contra-indications: it may be of benefit to some people, it may have very little effect, or it may even be harmful.

The CMHTs integrated within a locality's mental health service were deemed to be the most suitable "single post-box". The ease of access, the multiplicity of skills, and the coordination with primary care, secondary out-patient settings, and tertiary specialist services made the CMHTs an ideal portal of entry. In addition, according to the implementation guidelines, the CMHTs are supposed to provide generic and formal assessment and Type A and B treatments. However, some controversy still remains regarding different types of psychotherapy and the delivery thereof, as well as the mode of implementation and development across services. Meanwhile, most referrals will continue to be directed towards a Local Psychological Therapy Service (LPTS), even if the CMHTs become the "gatekeepers" of referrals.

It is argued that the single route has the dual advantage of greatly reducing the waiting time and minimizing multiple assessments. In spite of certain reservations, we are generally in agreement with the aims of this proposal. We believe that in order for this system to function effectively there is a need for greater cooperation between LPTS, CMHTs, and other mental health services, better channels of communication, equitable distribution of resources, and appropriate funding. Furthermore, power struggles, disrespect for each other's way of working, the question of ultimate responsibility for the care of the patient, and diffusion of roles will need to be addressed and worked with continuously.

Questionnaire

The use of pre-assessment and assessment questionnaires is not ubiquitous.

In our services, a pre-assessment questionnaire is sent together with the appointment letter. Our psychotherapy pre-assessment questionnaire is simple and descriptive and the patient is informed in the accompanying letter that refusal to complete such a questionnaire does not preclude the offer of an appointment. It is expected that patients will return the questionnaires in a prepaid envelope prior to their appointment, thus allowing the assessor to have some preliminary information prior to the assessment date. However, some patients may wish to fill out the questionnaire in the waiting room. In some services the questionnaires are completed during the assessment time.

Our pre-assessment questionnaires allow for the collection of subjective data including demographic information and past history. They provide space for self-reflection, expectations regarding treatment, and they also prepare the patient for the relatively unstructured orientation of the interview. The manner in which the questionnaires are completed, in particular any reluctance to fill them in, may reflect patients' feeling of anxiety, shame, and ambivalence when asked to disclose personal details in an impersonal way.

In our experience most patients tend to complete questionnaires. An audit of returned questionnaires found that patients who returned them were more likely to attend their first assessment interview (KG). In addition, the questionnaire provides useful information that can be elaborated upon during the assessment proper. However, some authors (Soutter & Garelick, 1999) called into question the usefulness of such pre-assessment questionnaires. More structured assessment questionnaires such as the Beck Depression Inventory (BDI), the Brief Symptom Inventory (BSI), and Clinical Outcomes in Routine Evaluation (CORE) should be used routinely and we believe that they will soon become an integral part of the assessment process in order to monitor outcome. These question-naires provide both a useful cut-off point for separating clinical from non-clinical cases and an indication of severity and risk. Moreover, they can be used to monitor psychotherapy progress. However, the usefulness of such structured tests in understanding a patient during a proper psychodynamic assessment is controversial, for most questions tend to be symptom-orientated and, according to some, "muddy the patient–assessor interaction".

Assessment attendance rate and waiting time

In a review article, Sharp & Hamilton (2001) examined the non-attendance rate for both general practice surgeries and out-patient clinics and reported that the percentages for non-attendance ranged from 5% to 34%. This is without doubt one of the major areas of waste in the NHS. They quoted studies indicating that youth, male gender, long waiting lists, and deprivation have been associated with poor hospital out-patient attendance, while non-attendance rates in psychiatry appear to be indicative of severity of illness. There is also some evidence that young age and length of waiting time can negatively influence the attendance rate for psychological therapies (Loumidis & Shropshire, 1997). However, when the effects of waiting time and age were controlled for, these authors found that patients with complex problems and patients who had never sought psychological treatment in the past were less likely to attend.

Some studies have shown that when the reason for referral is clearly explained and the patient agrees to be referred, he or she is more likely to attend a psychiatric clinic (Huws, 1992; Killaspy et al., 2000; Webster, 1992). Our own experience has shown that referrals from consultant psychiatrists, who tend to engage with the patient, are less prone to fail attending their first appointment. For example, the non-attendance (DNA) rate of patients referred by consultant psychiatrists to one of the authors (LC) for psychotherapy assess-ment was 7%, compared with 12% from general practitioners' refer-rals. It would seem that engaging with, and giving an explanation about, psychotherapy improves the opting-in process, but we are also well aware that general practitioners are very busy and may not have adequate time to explain. A number of studies have shown that addressing patients' concerns about their difficulties, rather than simply addressing their symptoms, may improve the engagement with other services (McCabe *et al.*, 2002; Roter *et al.*, 1995).

Collaboration between referrers and providers of psychological therapies is essential (Ross & Hardy, 1999). Lack of collaboration may be one of the reasons for patients failing to attend their first consultation. Furthermore, there is a need to identify and improve factors which may influence the mode of referral and the response from providers.

Attempts should be made to promote the understanding of psychological factors and to improve detection of such factors relevant to health. Education programmes, Balint type groups, and referral criteria are some examples that could help to refine the referral process. There is a need for further research to establish those factors that may impact on patient non-attendance to specialist services, e.g. preparation of patients by GP prior to referral.

The way in which a specialist psychological service responds to a patient following a referral may well be important in reducing the attrition rate.

In most services there is a variable length of time between the receipt of referral and the first appointment for assessment. This may be due to differences in available resources, quality of administration, whether or not there are clear pathways of referral, and first appointment procedures.

For a number of years our psychotherapy services have had two separate waiting lists: one for assessment and one for treatment. We have always endeavoured to keep the waiting time for assessment to between four and six weeks following the receipt of the referral letter and to "fast-track" patients with special needs whenever possible. After the initial assessment, patients deemed to be suitable for psychodynamic psychotherapy are placed on the relevant therapy waiting list where, according to resources, they often remain for between three and six months. During this period patients may drop out. In order to obviate this problem, we offer to see them from time to time.

We have identified a number of measures that have helped patients to keep their first appointment for assessment, and the following are some simple procedures that we have adopted.

- To send a letter asking whether the patient wishes to be offered an appointment (Appendix 1).
- To send a brief explanation of psychotherapy.
- To send a pre-assessment questionnaire (Appendix 2) along with an appointment letter.
- To request confirmation of attendance by reply slip (Appendix 3).
- To explain that if confirmation is not received within a certain time scale, the appointment will be given to somebody else.

These measures, which involve the patient's cooperation from the outset, have clearly helped with the issue of "opting in" for the assessment process; however, 10–20% of patients still fail to attend the first interview (Bateman, 2000; Caparrotta, 2000; Deane, 1993; Ghaffari, 2000). It may prove necessary to adopt additional measures such as crèche facilities, flexible working times and/or reminders (Nicholson, 1994) to reduce further the rate of non-attendance. In addition, we should not forget the invaluable role of an efficient and sympathetic secretary in reducing non-attendance rate.

To conclude, reasons for poor attendance are multiple and numerous and consequently there are no simple solutions. Reasons common to all NHS clinics may well co-exist with reasons peculiar to individual specialist services. In order to examine the latter reasons, detailed auditing is required.

CHAPTER THREE

Pre-specialist opinion

There is strong empirical evidence for the potential benefit of psychological treatments to individuals with a wide range of mental health problems (DoH, 2001), hence, psychological therapies should always be considered as an option when assessing such individuals.

The commencement of the assessment process sometimes predates the referral letter, because most patients referred to specialist local psychological therapy services will already have undergone a preliminary screening. That is to say, the referrer, whether in primary or secondary care, in making the referral is expressing the opinion that the patient may be helped psychotherapeutically. This preliminary phase, involving the formation of a "pre-specialist opinion" on the part of the referrer, as opposed to a "specialist assessment" conducted by psychological therapy specialists, is an important but little studied component of an overall assessment for psychological therapies. The referrer, in formulating an opinion, may already be asking any, or all, of the questions posed below.

Is psychological intervention the treatment of choice?

> Mr E, a teacher, consulted his GP because he had become so anxious that he could no longer function at work. The referring GP established through tactful questioning that Mr E was afraid of losing control of his anger. He was also able to elicit that past conflicts and sibling rivalry had re-surfaced when a colleague, much less experienced and junior to Mr E, was promoted to a position above him.

In the above vignette the sensitivity and clinical acumen of the GP allowed for an accurate screening of Mr E's difficulties, which led to an appropriate referral for assessment for psychological therapy.

Is psychological therapy an alternative to pharmacological therapy?

It is not uncommon for patients to refuse drug treatment, either from the outset or following an unsuccessful or problematic course of medication in the past. The reasons for such refusals are varied: planning for a family, the unpleasant effects of "feeling like a zombie", or "feeling detached or numb", the belief that medication interferes with the mind, and side effects perceived to be intolerable. Whenever possible, referrers tend to support the wishes of such patients and initiate a specialist psychological assessment referral.

However, there are situations where the referrer has already concluded that a psychotherapeutic intervention would not provide a suitable alternative to drug therapy, but may feel pressured by the patient and/or his/her relatives to revisit this decision.

> Mr K, suffering from a long-term schizophrenic illness, attended his psychiatric out-patient appointment with his relatives demanding psychotherapy. One of the relatives had read somewhere about the "dreadful effects" of medication and the benefits of psychotherapy. She had managed to convince Mr K and his family that medication was not necessary and his illness could be cured by psychotherapy alone. The psychiatrist was very concerned and tried to dissuade Mr K from stopping his medication and gave an explanation of why he did not consider psychotherapy alone to be appropriate for this condition. He reluctantly

agreed to a psychotherapy referral and a thorough assessment helped the patient and his relatives to be more realistic about their expectations of psychotherapy. Mr K agreed to continue with his prescribed medication alongside a task-orientated psychological intervention to help him to structure his daily life and deal better with his symptoms.

Nowadays, easily accessible information in the media and on the internet has led to better knowledge of the various forms of psychotherapy, but it has also given rise to unrealistic expectations and inappropriate requests for psychological therapies.

Is psychotherapy a suitable adjunct to other therapeutic modalities?

We believe that a holistic approach to the management of the patient is essential. Hence, the psychological perspective including personality development should always be included in any treatment planning (Perry *et al.*, 1987).

The following example illustrates how a multidisciplinary approach, taking into consideration the psychological perspective, can be helpful in the management of a patient in a CMHT.

Mr C, a man with a history of bipolar affective disorder, was referred by community psychiatric nurse (CPN) to the CMHT because he had relapsed a number of times over the preceding months, often requiring admission to hospital. Previously, his symptoms had been well managed by medication and no particular precipitants could fully account for the increase in hypomanic episodes.

The case was reviewed by the multidisciplinary team and it was decided that a thorough psychological assessment should be considered. The psychotherapist, who was invited to the case discussion, undertook the assessment. During the course of the assessment interview two important details emerged. First, that Mr C had a very active fantasy life in which he would live out sexual relationships with women caring for him. Second, that the newly allocated female CPN had become the secret focus of his attention. He had found it difficult to share his thoughts with anyone because he feared ridicule. However, the reason why he became so infatuated with this particular person did not become clear until a link was made with the caring role of an older

female cousin, resembling his nurse, who had introduced him to excit-
ing sexual games.

The psychological assessment allowed for a better understanding of Mr C's illness and helped to identify how powerful hidden
(unconscious) factors may limit the effect of medication in preventing relapse.

Following the assessment, Mr C was given the opportunity to
explore and work through the above issues with brief focal psychodynamic psychotherapy.

While in the past the combination of psychoanalytic psychotherapy and medication was often frowned upon, because it was
thought to interfere with the therapeutic relationship, it has now
become less of a controversial issue.

Is the patient's poor compliance with medication amenable to a psychological therapy intervention?

Mr A, an intelligent married man of fifty suffering from insulin-
dependent diabetes, was referred by the treating physician who sus-
pected that psychological factors had been contributing to Mr A's poor
response to treatment over the last two years. On several occasions his
wife had found him in a comatose state necessitating admission to
hospital.

In the course of a thorough psychotherapy assessment, Mr A admitted
to an affair of two years' duration. The assessor formed an hypothesis
that Mr A. had developed a maladaptive response to his guilt by
punishing himself through manipulation of his insulin. This was
confirmed later in the course of psychotherapy.

The above clinical vignette is an interesting example of how treatment compliance can be unwittingly sabotaged.

Is the clinical picture confounded by personality disturbance hampering therapeutic engagement?

Personality disorder is defined in the *Diagnostic and Statistical
Manual of Mental Disorders* (*DSM-IV*) as "an enduring pattern of

inner experience and behaviour that deviates markedly from the expectations of the individual's culture, is pervasive and inflexible, has an onset in adolescence or early adulthood, is stable over time, and leads to distress or impairment." Personality disorders are grouped into three clusters, according to characteristics such as "odd or eccentric", "dramatic or erratic", and "anxious or fearful". Those personality disorders (antisocial, borderline, histrionic, and narcissistic personality disorders) subsumed by Cluster B have increasingly become recognized as potentially treatable conditions. Individuals suffering from such personality disorders present frequently to mental health services. Their treatment poses thorny management dilemmas and consumes large amounts of already stretched resources. Such patients are notoriously difficult to treat and have attracted the attention of the media in recent times. It can be argued that the apparent increase in the presentation of personality disorders is due to rapidly changing and unpredictable socio-cultural influences, greater social mobility, and an increased readiness to accept diagnoses as specialist treatment becomes more readily available.

> Miss Y, a 24-year-old, single, unemployed woman was referred to a specialist psychotherapy service by her the fourth consultant psychiatrist. Her first contact with mental health services occurred in latency when severe anxiety set in and was associated with separating from her mother. The clinical picture gradually expanded to include obsessive behaviour, eating disorder, self-harm, and clinical depression. She had received a number of treatments, including medication, cognitive-behaviour therapy, intermittent supportive psychotherapy, and she had seen a number of junior doctors in training and other mental health professionals. Furthermore, her parents contributed to her difficulties by interfering and forcing a number of changes in the treating team. The assessment revealed a morbid preoccupation with rejection and unwitting enactment of separation anxiety with self-harm and withdrawal after any change in the staff, thus compounding the already precarious engagement. Eventually this patient was referred to a day patient psychotherapy unit, where a consistent, longer-term psychotherapeutic contract was set up.

Rapid staff turnover, brief interventions, lack of consistency, and unwitting collusion can easily add to the patient's persistent fear of rejection, thereby exacerbating the underlying problem.

This interesting case highlights the importance of a thorough assessment that pays particular attention to underlying personality development. Moreover, the assessor needs to have in mind the availability of local resources and knowledge of specialist units. In the above case, the assessor would have had from the referral letter and other sources information that should have allowed him or her to consider from the outset that a more structured therapeutic environment would have been necessary. The assessment, in fact, confirmed the need for such a facility. A recent document (National Institute of Mental Health (Executive) (NIMH(E)), 2003) underlines the importance of this and advocates the need to identify and/or develop multidisciplinary day services for personality disorders, particularly in areas of high morbidity (Snowden & Kane, 2003).

Can assessment help to unravel a therapeutic stalemate?

Mrs J, who suffered from refractory depression, had been under the care of a day hospital for the past eighteen months. A number of therapeutic interventions were tried with little success. Initial enthusiasm and therapeutic zeal gave way to feelings of frustration and impotence in the staff. The members of the treating team, anxious about their counterproductive responses, organized a referral to a psychotherapy service. The psychotherapy assessment identified the patient's deeply entrenched inner conflict with authority figures, which was enacted in the power struggle between the patient and the team.

A therapeutic stalemate can often lead to frustration and a deep sense of helplessness in the team and the patient. When not clearly understood, such a stalemate may lead to inappropriate treatment regimes contributing yet further to the underlying stagnation.

In this chapter, various clinical situations have been described which are intended to assist potential referrers in formulating more specifically their reasons for a specialist referral. This list is not exhaustive. It is important to note that the decision to refer may be influenced by the patient alone, the interaction between the patient and his/her relatives, or the interaction between the patient and the referrer.

CHAPTER FOUR

Specialist assessment

Once a decision has been made to refer the patient for a psychotherapy consultation, the specialist assessment proper begins.

To date, there is still a level of uncertainty as to what are the ingredients of a "good-enough" assessment. There is no clear-cut template for assessment and the format of assessment interviews may vary considerably from assessor to assessor.

Our assessment interview technique may reflect our own particular style and it is tailored to each patient according to his/her presenting problems and the nature of the interaction during the interview. While we tend to use a framework to structure the consultation, we also try to retain a flexible "listening ear" and pay particular attention to the nature and quality of the interaction.

Within our personal, structured framework the following questions are paramount.

(a) What are the patient's key problems and difficulties?
(b) Is psychological intervention a suitable form of treatment for this particular patient?
(c) Is the patient suitable for psychodynamic psychotherapy?

(d) If the patient is deemed suitable for psychodynamic psychotherapy what is then the psychodynamic formulation?

(e) What treatment modality, where, and by whom can the patient
best be helped?

If the patient is deemed unsuitable for psychological intervention,
a number of alternative options are considered and discussed with
the patient. We will touch upon these options in Chapter Eight.

Before beginning the consultation, we consider it essential and
courteous to introduce ourselves. This point may seem obvious, but
we would still like to stress it because, as previously stated, there
are still some practising clinicians who believe that a completely
silent reception on the part of the assessor is most helpful in developing an initial understanding of the patient's state of mind.

We also make it clear how long the interview will last, usually
between 1 and 1½ hours. We listen to and respect the patient's views
and try to give feedback in a way that is understandable (General
Medical Council, 2001).

What are the patient's key problems and difficulties? (i.e. listening , history taking, and clarifying the presenting problems)

Having introduced ourselves, we begin the consultation by asking
whether the patient knows why he/she has been referred for
psychological therapy. We then indicate that although we may
already have some knowledge of their difficulties from the referral
letter, questionnaires and/or previous notes, it would be helpful to
hear "their story" and concerns about their difficulties.

Although it is clearly stated in the appointment letter that the
appointment is for an assessment, some patients still arrive at the
consultation with expectations of commencing treatment. The
assessor, in our view, needs to regard the first encounter with the
patient as an assessment consultation and to clearly differentiate it
from a therapy session. As Schachter (1997) pointed out, the aim of
an assessment is not to engage the patient in a transference relationship, but to offer time and space where the patient can feel free
to talk about his/her difficulties, conflicts, and anxieties. This is

particularly relevant if the assessor is not the therapist, as is often the case in a busy psychological therapies service.

In order to dispel these erroneous expectations and any confusion between assessment and treatment, we make it clear from the outset. We also explain that we hope this assessment consultation will allow patients to clarify and discuss their presenting difficulties. Finally, we inform them that at the end of the consultation we hope to reach together a decision as to whether psychological therapy is the best way forward.

The referral letter may already contain a comprehensive background history that helps the assessor to focus on the presenting problem(s), conflicts, anxieties, and their meaning to the patient. In the previous chapter we elaborated upon the importance of the pre-specialist opinion, which can facilitate the initial phase of this specialist assessment.

We have also found that the use of preliminary questionnaires to collect subjective data can provide us with some indication of the severity of the problem, the person's capacity for self-reflection, and of his/her expectations of psychological treatment.

We have noticed at times that the urgency with which the patient has engaged the referrer may have subsided by the time of the assessment. This may allow for a more reflective initial contact, thus setting the path for self-scrutiny.

Listening and history taking

Each patient is considered as a unique entity with his/her individual life history. As we listen to the patient and ask relevant questions, we gather information that gradually allows us to form a picture of the person and his/her history. During this process we have specific questions in mind, as shown below.

- How does the patient subjectively perceive his/her own difficulties? (These may be different from the observers' perceptions.)
- Is the patient aware of meaningful links between the present problems and the past?
- Why is the patient coming for help at this particular time of his/her life (i.e. precipitants)?

- Why is this particular patient finding it difficult to function (i.e. vulnerability factors)?
- Are there any factors that are contributing to or maintaining the patient's difficulties (e.g. physical conditions)?
- Are there any risk factors involved (e.g. self harm and episodes of violence)?

We will now attempt to examine the above questions in the following case presentation.

> A general practitioner referred a successful 45-year-old solicitor for depression. Mr F could not understand how he had changed from being a sporty, popular, and energetic man to an anxious, insecure, "total wreck". He viewed himself in a wholly negative way which he realized was affecting his performance at work and his relationship with his friends and his only daughter. Colleagues at work continued to remark on his irritability and his intolerance of imperfections. His friends were concerned with his general withdrawal and lack of social contact.

Having paid particular heed to the patient's concerns, his subjective view of the presenting complaint, and the way in which it affects his daily functioning, we then try to identify the factors which have resulted in the patient seeking help at this particular stage of his life. The coherence with which Mr F. describes the presenting problem and the identification of the precipitating factors can also guide us to ask pertinent questions about the past (including medical and psychiatric history of both the patient and his extended family) and thus establish important connections.

> For the first twenty minutes of the interview, Mr F blamed the pressure of his work for his inability to cope. His reporting was very detailed but it left the assessor puzzled and unsure as to why Mr F had reacted in such an extreme way to pressures that he had dealt with adequately before. Therefore, the assessor attempted to identify the reasons why Mr F was finding it so difficult to cope with these pressures now. Eventually it emerged that two recent life events had had a major impact: the departure of a senior colleague and the imminent moving away of his only daughter, for whom he had cared single-handedly since he lost his wife two years previously. His wife, to whom he had been truly devoted, had died of cancer after many months of pain.

He nursed her as he had his mother before she died ten years previously.

Mr F was then able to link the departures of his colleague and his daughter with a number of exits in his own life. The major theme, therefore, was one of loss.

Having established that Mr F was able to self-reflect and to make some links between the present and the past, in the next stage of our history taking we try to identify developmental issues that have particular relevance and meaning to the presenting problems. We would be looking, for example, at relationships with family and friends. We try to get a flavour of early memories and the nature and meanings of early interactions.

Mr F described a difficult relationship with a strong, draconian mother, with whom he fought a great deal. On recalling his early childhood, Mr F talked with great clarity of an experience that affected him at the age of three, when he was admitted to hospital for a minor ailment. He remembered painful feelings of abandonment by his mother in an empty ward. Not long afterwards, he was farmed out to family friends when his mother needed to be hospitalized. He developed, therefore, an anxious attachment to his mother, whom he perceived as abandoning and uncaring, which might explain his vulnerability to loss.

Having clarified the presenting problems, recent precipitants, and relevant vulnerability factors, we try to identify whether there are other issues that contributed to the severity of Mr F's reaction.

He described his relationship with his father as idyllic, but said that it turned sour after the birth of his brother when Mr F was five. He had always harboured the idea that his father preferred his younger son to him, which made it difficult for Mr F to develop a close relationship with his brother. Nevertheless, there was a clear longing to be loved and noticed by his father, although the rage triggered by the shame of being sidelined by him was never very far from the surface.

When the assessor mentioned his possible anger towards the senior colleague who had left the firm, Mr F made the connection to his father and was surprised at the ease with which the denied pent-up anger surfaced. These recent events had reawakened his unresolved feelings of mourning in relation to both parents.

In attempting to understand a patient, we look not only at why he/she is not functioning well, but also we explore achievements and positive coping mechanisms (attachments, successful early relationships, etc.). Unfortunately, there is a tendency in our profession to become blasé and to look only for signs and symptoms of underlying psychopathology, thereby running the risk of overlooking the more positive and healthy aspects of the patient's functioning. We believe that by drawing attention to these more positive features, we will enable the patient to become less frightened and less ashamed and, possibly, more likely to cooperate with the interviewing process.

Mr F, in fact, looked markedly relieved when at one point during the interview the assessor highlighted some positive aspects of his life and remarked on his strength in keeping himself going.

Although Mr F had entertained fleeting ideas of suicide, a thorough risk assessment revealed that he no longer had active suicidal ideation and his seeking help contained an element of hope.

This case illustrates how the patient's capacity to deal with his or her problems in an appropriate manner depends on the subjective severity of the precipitant(s). After all, every individual has a different threshold. Furthermore, this case demonstrates how the patient's developmental history has clearly influenced and shaped his responses.

Diagnostic assessment

We firmly believe that a diagnostic assessment is an essential component of any comprehensive assessment for psychotherapy.

Diagnostic assessment, an important component of case formulation, is a process by which signs and symptoms are identified and assigned to a disease entity, thus enabling us to make predictions about treatment, prognosis and, as we shall see, risk considerations. For example, in the assessment of young people and children for psychodynamic psychotherapy, diagnostic factors have been found to be important as predictors for suitability for psychotherapy (Target & Fonagy, 1994). However, we would like to stress that diagnosis constitutes only a part of an overall clinical assessment, and on its own should not dictate recommendations for treatment suitability.

There have been many attempts to classify mental disorders according to phenomenology, aetiology, and defining features, which have led over the years to the development of a number of differing classifications systems. The *International Classification of Diseases* (*ICD*) developed by the World Health Organization, and its variant devised by the American Psychiatric Association, the *Diagnostic and Statistical Manual of Mental Disorders* (*DSM*), are the most widely used diagnostic systems in general psychiatry. They have been continuously revised and current versions are *ICD-10* and *DSM-IV*. Furthermore, their coding systems are now converging.

Traditionally, a categorical model has been the preferred mode of psychiatric disorder classification: that is, the division of psychiatric disorders into a number of separate and mutually exclusive categories such as schizophrenia, depression, neurosis, etc. A more comprehensive mode of classification is multidimensional (multiaxial system, *DSM*), whereby clinical presentations are based on the quantification of attributes across separate categories of functioning. This model of classification has the advantage of being more flexible, and does not tend to pigeonhole an individual into any single distinct entity.

A multiaxial system (*DSM-IV*, 1994) thus provides a number of dimensions including clinical disorders (Axis I), personality disorders (Axis II), general medical conditions (Axis III), psychosocial and environmental problems (Axis IV), as well as the global assessment of functioning (Axis V). Moreover, the *DSM-IV* places greater emphasis on cultural issues that are, as mentioned previously, becoming increasingly relevant.

The above model of classification can also be more easily applied to a psychotherapeutic assessment because it combines descriptive and observed clinical disorders with personality functioning and other dimensions.

The *DSM-IV* offers distinct advantages over previous monolithic systems of classification; it provides both a useful framework and a conventional way of communicating our findings and continues to be a major tool for mental health research, including psychotherapy research (Wilson, 1993). One should not forget, however, that it remains a tool of considerable limitations and that some authors have gone as far as claiming that terms in psychiatry, psychopathology, and psychoanalysis amount to nothing more than metaphors (Gelder & Lopez-Llbor, 2000; Gozzetti & Sava, 2001), while diagnostic categories may create an illusion of homogeneity (Roth & Fonagy, 1996).

In reaching a diagnosis, it is important to avoid focusing on the manifest symptoms alone. It is pertinent to consider those symptoms as a form of communication within the context of different dimensions, including developmental and personality factors, social culture, and environmental conditions (Campbell & Russell, 1983; Pazzagli & Rossi Monti, 1999). For example, a depressive episode as a diagnostic category is a form of communication, but it will have different implications for the management and prognosis according to whether it can be linked to a medical condition, related to work, or to being the result of a loss.

The severity of the presenting problem is always an important variable to consider, particularly when deciding both the type and the length of psychological intervention. A number of reviews have reported poor treatment response when the presenting symptoms have been severe (Garfield, 1994; Lambert & Anderson, 1996; Luborsky et al. 1988). Shapiro et al. (1994), in a study of depressed patients treated either with CBT or dynamic interpersonal psychotherapy, found that both treatments were effective but those patients with more severe depressions improved more with the sixteen psychodynamic interpersonal sessions than with the eight CBT sessions.

Co-morbidity will also have an impact on diagnostic assessment and choice of treatment in that, while the treated condition may improve, the untreated condition may continue or even get worse (Brown & Barlow, 1992; Salomon et al., 1992). For example, patients with an eating disorder with co-morbid personality disorder have poorer outcome than patients without (Coker et al., 1993). Certain types of personality disorder also appear to influence the outcome. Schizotypal, borderline, and avoidant personality disorders predict a poorer outcome than that predicted for patients who present with a histrionic or dependent personality disorder (Turner, 1987). In addition, accurate and differential diagnosis will also help to ascertain the level of priority of intervention, particularly in the management of complex conditions such as personality disorders. Such disorders may necessitate a more integrated approach and/or careful considerations of issues such as whether or not medication or other forms of intervention should be used in the first instance.

Another major issue pertinent to diagnostic evaluation is that of misdiagnosis. It is not uncommon, for example, to under- or over-estimate the severity of psychopathology in the initial encounter. In the Menninger study (Wallerstein, 1986) there was an underestimation of profundity and severity of psychopathology, which became apparent only in the course of treatment, in some 60% of patients. Misdiagnosis can lead to recommendations for a treatment that is clearly unsuitable for the patient or that requires a commitment and intensity that the patient cannot sustain. These considerations are of particular relevance to the psychodynamic setting.

Risk assessment

Risk assessment is an essential component of a diagnostic assessment. By risk assessment we mean the screening and the appropriate management of risk factors such as deliberate self-harm, suicidality, risk to and from others, and self-neglect. Risk inherent to specific psychopathological traits of the patient, previous history of violence to self and others, the current circumstances, and the likelihood of acting-out within the therapeutic process needs to be evaluated. Any potential danger to the prospective therapist (and, indeed, assessors) should never be underestimated.

> An inexperienced assessor conducted a psychological assessment of a security guard. As the patient was very suspicious and reticent about disclosing personal details, she found the interview extremely difficult. She eventually decided that it was appropriate to have a further consultation. When she brought the first assessment to supervision with a senior clinician, it was suggested that she should ask the patient whether, being a security guard, he was carrying a gun. On the second consultation the patient indeed proudly revealed that he always carried a gun.

In the light of the fact that for some patients the referral to psychological therapy services represents their first portal of entry to mental health services, the assessor should also be aware of his/her potential role as care coordinator within the Care Programme Approach (CPA). This includes an assessment of risk, a written care plan, and relevant contact numbers for use in case of emergency. Those patients who have had previous contact with mental heath services and those on enhanced level should have additional regular reviews by multidisciplinary health teams. These safety measures, involving patients and staff, should always be revised and at the forefront of any psychotherapy assessment. For example, there is now robust evidence indicating that patients who have attempted suicide, even if in the remote past, pose a serious suicidal risk (Jenkins *et al.*, 2002; Runeson, 2002).

A number of important questions, regarding the conducting of a risk assessment within a psychotherapy consultation, demand to be addressed. Within the context of risk assessment, the awareness of counter-transference[1] feelings is an invaluable tool. Is this patient, who appears calm and composed, concealing a revengeful, aggressive component? Can we be sure that an attempted suicide is the result of a clinical depressive illness? Has the patient attempted suicide before? Could self-neglect represent the tip of an iceberg and obscure instead the onset of a schizophrenic condition? Would this patient be best managed in a multidisciplinary setting (enhanced CPA)?

> Mr D was referred to the psychological therapy services by his general practitioner for what appeared to be a clear-cut depressive condition exacerbated by several operations on his arm after being bitten by a dog. A number of predisposing, precipitating, and perpetuating factors clearly pointed to a diagnosis of depression. However, an experienced assessor, who was not happy with accepting the diagnosis of depression because he sensed something dangerous unfolding during the consultation, undertook painstaking and careful probing. Eventually it was possible to identify some hidden and worrying aspects, including a relentless, murderous rage towards his girlfriend for having betrayed him, and long-harboured feelings of revenge towards authority figures. The patient had an extensive forensic and drug history, having been in prison for a variety of offences.

This rather extreme example illustrates how relevant information can be missed, if consideration is given only to presenting symptoms and problems during a psychotherapy assessment, without due attention to underlying risk factors. In the case of Mr D, who was placed on an enhanced CPA, psychotherapy could only be considered in a safe setting (e.g. forensic psychotherapy units) with an appropriate, experienced psychotherapist who had full knowledge of the danger that this patient might pose during a course of psychotherapy. If such a setting could not be identified, it would be inappropriate to consider psychotherapy of any kind.

During an initial assessment some patients tend to conceal, wittingly or unwittingly, certain aspects of their behaviour, symptoms, and personality traits. This may be due to conscious withholding, as in the case of Mr D, shame, fear of stigmatization, rejection, or even fear of hospitalization. Typical examples of this might include some patients who abuse alcohol, anorexic patients who use a variety of subterfuges to conceal the extent of their weight loss, patients suffering from schizophrenia who conceal the presence of auditory hallucinations, and patients with extended forensic and drug history with a tendency to deceive. The Menninger study (Wallerstein, 1958) found surprising evidence that 55% of their patients had in fact concealed highly relevant information, which only became available by gradually developing a trusting relationship in therapy.

If there are reasons to suspect withholding of information, a way to obviate some of the above difficulties is to interview relatives or relevant close friends. This procedure may throw further light on the patient's life history and personality development.

Having stressed the importance of diagnosis and risk assessment, our experience has also taught us to be aware of their pitfalls and limitations. Beside the problem of misdiagnosis and withholding of information, we want to emphasize that our initial diagnosis and risk assessment can only be provisional. As Pazzagli & Rossi Monti (1999) pointed out: "[Diagnosis] is a point of departure, not a point of arrival". In other words, we should always be prepared to review our original diagnostic considerations as they may well change over time and during the course of treatment.

The relevance of provisional diagnosis and how it dovetails with a psychodynamic formulation will be addressed at a later stage.

This chapter is not intended to provide readers with conventional psychiatric diagnoses, but rather we urge all those practising talking therapies to acquaint themselves with psychiatric nosology and risk assessment.

In summary, the use of diagnosis in the assessment of patients for psychological therapies has its advantages and disadvantages. On the one hand it may place too much emphasis on symptoms alone, without paying attention to the meaning of the presenting problems, the uniqueness of the individual, and the relationship between the assessor and that particular patient. On the other hand, elucidating personality variables, severity of symptoms, and other co-morbid conditions are important in the planning of treatment.

Note

1. For definition of counter-transference see page 58.

CHAPTER FIVE

Suitability for psychological therapy

I n this chapter we will continue with our structured plan by exploring, thinking, developing, and testing hypotheses with the patient, in order to arrive at an answer to a question raised in the previous chapter.

Is psychological intervention a suitable form of treatment for this particular patient?

Appropriate selection of patients for psychological therapy and, in particular, for psychodynamic psychotherapy, is essential. Poor selection may have deleterious effects on patients, and can also lead to a considerable waste of limited resources. Truant (1998) states that on average some 25% of patients will drop out of therapy prematurely, and about 50% of these do so within the first four weeks.

Two well-known generic suitability factors, which in our opinion underpin any form of talking therapy, will now be considered. These are:

(i)   motivation to change;
(ii) capacity to form a working (therapeutic) relationship.

It is important to carry out a detailed and careful assessment of these two factors. Our own clinical experience confirms the general view that lack of motivation and poor therapeutic relationship probably account for the vast majority of drop-out cases.

Motivation to change

We believe that the extent to which a person is motivated to change is an important factor to be considered when attempting to reach a decision regarding suitability for any type of psychological therapy. Motivation is a highly complex, dynamic concept, which may fluctuate before and during treatment.

Rosenbaum *et al.* (1997) provide a helpful definition of motivation as: "The ability to discern inner causes, which has maintained the patient's request for a referral". They also consider sincerity, depth, and non-compulsiveness of the wish to change to be important factors.

Appelbaum (1972) identifies three closely related subdivisions of motivation:

the wish to get help;
the wish to change;
the wish to continue treatment.

Schulte-Markwort *et al.* (1999), in their work with children and adolescents, differentiated between global motivation for change and motivation for psychotherapeutic treatment.

Motivation to change involves not only the search for symptomatic relief, but also the capacity to acknowledge distress, a certain degree of curiosity, and an ability or willingness to explore the underlying reasons for that distress with a view to preventing future recurrence of symptoms.

The following clinical vignettes illustrate different levels of motivation to change.

Mrs B was referred by her general practitioner. She had recently discovered her husband's infidelity and a marital crisis ensued, which resulted in the husband leaving home. Mrs B's main wish was to get help from professionals in order to ensure her husband's return. During the crisis she did not express any curiosity to examine herself or the relationship, but simply pined for her husband's return.

Mrs J, a 36-year-old, highly successful bank manager, sought help for a long-standing instability in her mood. After many years of "putting up with" the symptoms of low and elated moods she finally decided that she wanted a "more normal life". Initially her psychiatrist offered her medication, but Mrs J was not satisfied with a temporary "cure". Rather, she was keen to understand the reasons for her instability of mood and through this understanding attempt to prevent future relapses. During the assessment Mrs J not only demonstrated a desire for symptomatic relief, but she also showed curiosity about the meaning of these symptoms and the possibility of learning strategies for their prevention.

It is not unusual to discover during assessment that the principal motivation for attendance does not stem from the patient. Freud (1905) himself believed that "people who are not driven to seek treatment by their own sufferings, but who submit to it only because they are forced to by the authority of relatives" were not suitable for psychoanalytic treatment. The referral for a psychological therapy assessment may be initiated by a wish to please and/or a need dictated by a family member, whose life at times has been made impossible, or by a friend or member of the helping professions, who may have a rather different agenda (Klauber, 1986).

Young children do not have an accurate conception of change, while adolescents tend to minimize dysfunctions, to be less likely to report difficulties, and to be less aware of the impact of their behaviour on others. Consequently, parents or other adults may appropriately instigate the referral. In young people, a strong motivation for treatment may also be confused with motivation to change, thus obscuring a need for temporary containment. In some cases, the provision of containment serves to reduce any initial urgency and may not be followed by further treatment if a strong resistance to change becomes apparent (Caparrotta, 1997).

In addition, motivation for change can be influenced by secondary gains. Patients may present themselves with an apparent strong wish for treatment, but on careful assessment and at times only during the actual therapy, it becomes clear that the motivation is driven, for example, by financial gains, social benefits, court proceedings, and/or other ulterior motives.

Some older adults may become motivated to seek treatment only when they acknowledge that this may be their last chance to change.

Motivation to change is obvious during the assessment in some patients. For other patients, for example those suffering from substance abuse and eating disorders, who might initially be classified as unmotivated to change, tactful exploration, clarification of underlying fears, and the use of pre-treatment strategies to enhance motivation may increase their wish to seek treatment and change (Feld et al., 2001; Miller et al., 1993).

Furthermore, information about previous experience in psychological therapies and how and why the therapy was terminated may shed further light on the patient's motivation.

In exploring motivation to change, we have found particular probes to be useful. Examples include questions such as "What do you expect from therapy?", "How do you think it will help you?" and "What has led you to seek help at this particular stage of your life?", or "You told me that you became aware of your difficulties some years ago. What stopped you from seeking help then and what makes you want to change now?"

> Ms E, a 22-year-old computer programmer, was referred by her general practitioner because of abnormal eating habits, following repeated contacts with the surgery on the part of her boyfriend. During the assessment Ms E revealed that her partner had also approached her occupational health representative for help on several occasions. On closer questioning it became apparent that the problems had in fact been present for the last four to five years, but Ms E had only come now as she found her boyfriend's constant nagging intolerable and was frightened of losing her job. She had reluctantly agreed to come as a way of pleasing her boyfriend, but she made it clear from the outset that she did not wish to stop binge eating. However, on further exploration she was able to link the bingeing to a difficult relationship with her mother. This linking allowed her to verbalize her wish for a better

relationship with her mother and enabled her to acknowledge the need for further exploration.

Motivation paves the way for the formation of therapeutic alliance and may prevent early drop out from treatment (Rosenbaum & Horowitz, 1983), particularly in young people (Kazdin *et al.*, 1993). There is some evidence for the relationship between initial assessment of motivation to change and treatment outcome (Bergin & Garfield, 1994; Høglend, 1996; Keithly *et al.*, 1980; Malan, 1979). Patients who are highly motivated from the outset tend to do better in brief psychoanalytic psychotherapy and group psychotherapy (Horowitz *et al.*, 1984; Sifneos, 1979; Yalom, 1995).

It is also our clinical experience that those patients who have a very strong motivation to change at the outset tend to remain in treatment. In our view, preparatory work in order to enhance and foster realistic expectations, particularly with patients unaccustomed to introspection, may be rewarding. More rigorous research in this field is clearly necessary.

Capacity to form a working relationship

In any form of psychotherapy, the capacity to form a working relationship implies the willingness of the patient to accept and engage in the tasks and goals of therapy. This, in our view, is distinct from the therapeutic alliance, which refers to the quality and nature of the relationship between patient and therapist.

Freud was well aware of the importance of the contract ("pact") between the analyst and the patient working together towards a common goal. This contract requires active participation, commitment, and mutual collaboration with the therapist. Indeed, this capacity is a fundamental component of any effective psychotherapy (DoH, 2001; Wright & Davis, 1994).

There is some evidence that those patients who form an active and positive engagement from the outset are more likely to improve (Sotsky *et al.*, 1991). Moreover, patients' expectations of improvement have been found to be one of the predictors of full recovery (Meyer *et al.*, 2002).

In order to lay the foundations for commitment to a mutually agreed therapeutic plan, it is important to elucidate and immediately confront any expectations of "magical solutions" entertained by the patient.

> Miss G, a young, busy executive, developed phobic anxiety symptoms after a presentation at a conference, which led to avoidance of speaking in public. Recently, however, she had been promoted to a position where she was required to give weekly presentations to the executive board of her company. During the preceding five years she had worked extremely hard to gain this promotion, but was scared that she might lose her position because of her fears. At the end of the assessment, the need for her active participation and commitment was discussed. Even though there was a very real risk of losing her job, Miss G was reluctant to invest the commitment and time necessary to enable her to achieve her desired goal. It was clear that there was no willingness on the part of Miss G to engage in psychotherapy requiring active collaboration. The option of medication was then discussed and Miss G agreed to try this. The assessor was not satisfied with the outcome, but as the patient was unwilling to return for a second consultation, she was discharged. However, a few months later she was re-referred, and on that occasion she showed a strong motivation to participate in the therapeutic process.

The working relationship concerns participation and commitment in working with set tasks and goals. It should not be examined in isolation, for outcome depends on a combination of many variables, including the relationship between the assessor and the patient. It is not unusual for patients to agree to a general commitment to the psychotherapeutic process, but then make a conscious decision regarding the specific modality and person they wish to engage with.

In the NHS, the assessor is not necessarily the therapist. The confirmation during assessment that a patient is willing to undertake the task of psychotherapy does not necessarily mean that the patient will form a good therapeutic relationship with the therapist.

In conclusion, motivation and ability to form a working relationship are the minimum requirements for suitability for any psychotherapeutic intervention. With a picture of the patient in mind, and having established suitability, it may now be appropriate to proceed with a specialist psychodynamic exploration.

CHAPTER SIX

Psychodynamic assessment

I n the previous chapter we examined the two main generic suit-ability factors: motivation for change and the capacity to form a working relationship, which in our opinion are prerequisites of any form of talking therapy. In this chapter we will concentrate extensively on additional factors, which as we will see, are pivotal in assessing suitability for psychodynamic psychotherapy.

Psychodynamic assessment is an attempt to collate historical data and to reach a diagnostic formulation with the patient in order to understand the meaning of the presenting complaints. These complaints are now going to be considered in the context of the patient's emotional and personality development, including his/her fears, conflicts, and defensive structures elicited within the interaction between the patient and the assessor.

As psychodynamic assessment involves also the understanding of the patient's earlier relationships, the assessor, by virtue of his/her training and experience, should focus on aspects of these rela-tionships, which may be unconsciously repeated in the assessment process. An unconscious, albeit distorted, repetition based on past relationships will re-occur (be transferred) within the interaction between patient and assessor. These repetitions, which take place in all relationships to greater or lesser extent, Freud (1893) named "transference". Some authors (Thomä & Kächele, 1987) would argue that transference may indeed develop even prior to an assessment consultation.

Similarly, the assessor needs to monitor his/her own feelings elicited during the interaction with the patient and constantly try to distinguish what belongs to him/her from that belonging to the patient. For example, the assessor needs to question himself/herself as to whether his/her feeling of frustration with the slowness and tone of voice of the patient is due to the patient's particular presentation, or the assessor's need to hurry the consultation because of an important engagement, or perhaps even a combination of the two. This dynamic process, which was originally termed by Freud "counter-transference", has become another essential tool in psychodynamic psychotherapy.

Nowadays, many forms of psychotherapy acknowledge the existence of these processes, but the exclusive use of transference and counter-transference in assessment and psychotherapy distinguishes psychodynamic psychotherapy (and psychoanalysis) from other forms of psychotherapy.

As aspects of transference tend to occur in any relationship, we are firm believers that every clinician should be prepared to at least acknowledge the importance of its existence. A recently published Royal College of Psychiatrists Council Report (2002) on good clinical practice states: "The clinician should develop self-awareness—the ability to monitor and understand one's own feelings and actions within a therapeutic relationship." In our opinion, formalized training in psychodynamic principles for psychiatric trainees that allows such an ability to develop must be an integral part of their general psychiatric training.

Is the patient suitable for psychodynamic psychotherapy?

In order to assess the suitability of a patient for psychodynamic psychotherapy a number of concepts that together constitute the structure of a psychodynamic assessment will now be examined.

Traditionally, assessment of suitability for psychodynamic psychotherapy has focused on three principal areas:

(1) capacity to think psychologically (psychological mindedness);
(2) ego strength;
(3) capacity to form a therapeutic relationship.

Capacity to think psychologically (psychological mindedness)

As previously mentioned, the essence of psychodynamic assessment for suitability is to ascertain the patient's ability to understand
the meaning of his/her presenting complaints. This capacity has
been at times loosely referred to as psychological mindedness.
There have been a number of attempts to define this important
concept. For example, the capacity for psychological mindedness
has been defined as a capacity for self-exploration and the ability
to understand people and their problems in psychological terms
(Coltart, 1988; Piper *et al.*, 1998; Sandler *et al.*, 1992; Tyson & Sandler,
1971). According to Appelbaum (1973), psychological mindedness
includes the acknowledgement of connections between symptoms,
events, feelings, and thoughts, as well as "the goal of learning, the
meanings and the causes of the person's experiences and behaviour." Schafer (1970) includes the ability to observe elements of
tragedy and irony in one's own narrative. Psychological mindedness can also be summarized as the ability (curiosity) to identify
components of intra-psychic conflict.

However, a point that demands further clarification is to what
extent this capacity is innate, acquired, or inhibited by psychological conflicts, and to what extent it is culturally influenced.

In our experience, the apparent lack of this capacity does not
mean that there is an absolute deficit. In some patients it is possible
to encourage and develop such skills. For example, group work can
be helpful in fostering such a capacity through learning (Goldberg,
1994). Other authors (McCallum & Piper, 1990) have advocated the
use of simulated patient–therapist interactions on videotape in
the assessment procedure in order to gauge later patients' psychological mindedness.

The capacity to think psychologically is easily and immediately
recognizable in some patients during assessment. In others, when
this is not easily discernible, a more active questioning style is
required. Certain exploratory questions can be helpful in enabling

the patient to reflect and begin to make some useful links; for example, "Can you clarify what you mean by . . .?", "Any ideas as to why you feel such and such . . .?", and "Do you think that what you are talking about now has any connection with the experiences that you described earlier?"

> Mr A, a 35-year-old accountant, found it extremely difficult to talk about himself, except for repeating that he was depressed and not aware of any reasons for it. After a long interview, the assessor, who had tried very hard to tease out Mr A's capacity to show curiosity about himself, was reaching a conclusion that Mr A was not psychologically minded. However, when he pointed out that he had previously mentioned that his oldest brother had died of cancer, aged 35, some ten years ago, Mr A burst into tears and expressed how he had been constantly preoccupied by death for the previous few months. He then went on to talk for the first time about his feelings regarding his brother's death and its impact on his own life and that of his parents.

At times, an external event or physical ailment can trigger a wish for introspection and understanding.

> Mrs Y, a divorced woman of fifty, consulted her general practitioner because of headaches and palpitations. During the consultation, the general practitioner diagnosed a markedly elevated blood pressure and this was confirmed over a number of readings. She returned a month later overtly anxious and agitated and revealed to him that the discovery of her high blood pressure had had a major impact on her during the preceding month. She began for the first time to consider the importance of her life experiences in relation to her symptoms. She was very keen to understand and asked to be referred to the local psychological therapy services.

It is also important to be aware that certain cultures are more inclined towards psychological curiosity than others and different cultures have different ways of expressing their emotional problems. For example, Kakar (1985) warns us that most Indian patients do not link their problems to their life history, but tend to view them as coming from outside or as products of a previous life. Bernal et al. (1998) have also stressed that results from research on the efficacy and effectiveness of psychotherapy cannot be generalized easily to ethnic minorities.

In a psychodynamic assessment, so-called trial interpretations can also be used to ascertain the degree of psychological minded-ness and to test the capacity for therapeutic alliance. There is some controversy about the use of trial interpretations during assessment and more in particular transference interpretations (i.e. direct comments about a particular mode of relating to the assessor being reminiscent of past relationships with significant figures).

However, trial interpretations, when offered tentatively and sensitively, can be very helpful in enabling the patient to think in a different way and to stimulate his/her curiosity. This may lead to new understanding and further exploration initiated by the patient. Interpretations introduced by phrases "I wonder if . . .", or "Do you think that . . ." can be useful in enhancing the patient's capacity to think psychologically about his/her predicament and to make links between the presenting symptoms and the internal world.

On the other hand, since transference interpretations may lead to the development of powerful transference feelings, we need to be mindful of the danger of patients breaking down while waiting for treatment. This is particularly relevant when assessing vulnerable and fragile young patients (Rosenbluth & Yalom, 1997).

Dreams, which can be recurrent, day-dreams, fragments of dreams or nightmares can also be helpful in assessing the patient's curiosity and willingness to explore his/her inner world.

Various attempts have been made to assess and standardize psychological mindedness and over the years a number of scales have been developed. Piper et al. (1994) suggest that patients who score highly on psychological mindedness are more likely to benefit from psychodynamic psychotherapy. The validity and reliability of their findings are, however, still in question (Conte & Ratto, 1997; McCallum & Piper, 1997; Shill & Lumley, 2002). A recent study evaluating the relationship between psychological mindedness and outcome supports the importance of this vari-able for predicting good outcome in short-term psychotherapy (McCallum et al., 2003).

In conclusion, psychological mindedness, although clouded by controversies, remains a useful and important area to explore in a psychodynamic assessment. Further research is clearly needed in order to refine such an essential concept.

Ego strength

For the sake of clarity, ego (often used interchangeably with the notion of the self) can best be defined as a system of functions. Its main function is to integrate, adapt and provide a balance between one's own internal world and the outside world. It therefore mediates in an adaptive way between the individual and external reality. As the ego organizes and provides a sense of coherence, it lays the foundation for the development of the personality.

The ego is a dynamic concept. Its development constitutes a continuum from infancy to adult life. Because the ego has to negotiate through infinite conflicts arising from the delicate interplay between the environment and the internal world, it is subject to disturbances throughout this process. Genetic, intrauterine, and psychological predisposing factors greatly influence the development of the ego. The strength of the ego depends on failures, deficits, mastery, and success.

As the strength of the ego determines our capacity to deal in an adaptive manner with internal and external demands, it is an important concept to consider, from a clinical point of view, when assessing patients for psychodynamic psychotherapy. Wallerstein (1965), in discussing suitability, aptly remarks, "sick enough to need it and healthy enough to stand it".

A number of components will now be considered which have been traditionally grouped under the rubric of ego strength. These include:

(i)   relationship to reality (reality testing);
(ii)   quality of object relationships;
(iii) affective capacity;
(iv)   frustration tolerance and impulse control.

Relationship to reality

The concept "relationship to reality" includes a number of complex functions of the ego, at times used interchangeably (Moore & Fine, 1990). These are sense of reality, reality testing, and adaptation to reality.

One's own *sense of reality* can be described as the subjective awareness that internal and external perceptions are not imaginary and are consistent with one's own experiences. *Reality testing* is commonly referred to as the automatic and unconscious counterpart. The ego reality testing function involves a constant scanning between internal and external experiences, including their psychic representations. To put it in another way, these functions determine one's ability to evaluate situations and experiences as conforming to how the world actually is and to differentiate between inner and outer experiences.

The following clinical vignette illustrates an extreme example of severe impairment of reality testing, which also tested the skills of the assessor.

> Mr X was referred by his general practitioner, who wrote a brief referral letter indicating his agreement with the patient's wish to receive psychotherapy. Mr X attended the assessment interview looking dishevelled and menacing. Even before the assessor had an opportunity to make the customary introductory remarks Mr X launched into a fierce tirade. The tone of the presentation increased to a crescendo conveying his long-standing rage "against every single aspect of this messy world". It reached its peak when he shouted, "Why has the system not done anything to solve this?" He then proceeded by saying that he preferred his own company rather than "that" company and how he needed to cleanse himself by making sure that he eats the right food.

> Given the state of arousal of the patient, it was difficult for the assessor to say anything meaningful without sparking off a violent confrontational outburst. It became clear that even though Mr X had come seeking "psychotherapy", he had such a distorted perception of reality that he was prevented from acknowledging the presence of the assessor, let alone considering any other viewpoint.

Adaptation to reality refers to the individual's capacity to adapt psychologically and behaviourally to a given environment and to find adequate solutions to previously judged situations. Hartmann (1958) writes, "adaptation may come about by changes, which the individual effects in his environment (use of tools, technology in the widest sense of word, etc.), as well as appropriate changes in the psychophysical system." Hartmann's view of adaptation includes both intrapsychic adaptation and adaptation to the social and inter-personal environment and is not merely a passive acceptance of the demands of the socio-political world (Sandler & Dreher, 1996).

Impairments in any or all of these three functions, i.e. sense of reality, reality testing, and adaptation to reality, may lead to disrup-tions in the patient's relationship with reality, ranging from minor complaints and disturbances in the personality structure to major psychiatric symptomatology and personality disorders.

At times, the patient may present himself/herself in such a peculiar manner that the reality testing can be easily inferred from the outset.

The following two clinical sketches give a flavour of such modes of presentation.

> A female patient insisted on being interviewed standing up. The reason for this insistence became clear towards the end of the assessment when the assessor discovered that her need to stand up was related to her delusional belief that by sitting down she would deform her spine.

> A male patient came to the assessment wearing swimming trunks. When questioned about his attire, he remarked, ". . . I came to see a psychotherapist, not a vicar!"

Adaptation can be protective and influenced by socio-cultural factors. The assessor needs to balance the benefit of a psychothera-peutic intervention against the need to maintain a psychic equilib-rium, even if the level of disturbance is quite severe. For example, within certain relationships and/or family dynamics, an individual may have found the best adaptive solution even though it may appear dysfunctional to the assessor. Therefore, it is imperative to inform the patient from the outset that psychodynamic psychother-apy will inevitably challenge and possibly lead to change in the equilibrium of his/her relationships. If necessary, alternative forms of treatment may then be considered.

Quality of object relationships

The term "object" refers to a mental representation of an actual person. Object relationships can therefore be defined as the ability to respond and relate to others as real, whole people - differentiated from the self. Piper *et al.* (1998) define the quality of object relationships as referring to ". . . a person's lifelong pattern of relationships, identified on a dimension ranging from primitive to mature." The development of these patterns of relationships can be traced back to infancy. The quality of these early attachments shapes the nature of future relationships with others. Bowlby (1988) classified attachments as: secure, anxious–ambivalent, anxious–avoidant and disorganized. Since then various research studies have refined instruments to measure the nature of attachment. This is particularly important because it would appear that attachment style and quality affect treatment (Fonagy *et al.*, 1996; Meyer *et al.*, 2001).

The assessor can glean information about the patient's internal object relations from contextual examination of both past and current relationships, in addition to those relationships developing during the assessment itself, in order to identify patterns that are being repeated (Gabbard, 2000; Pine, 1990). Examples of these patterns are: Does the patient always need to please? What were the nature and extent of early bonds (attachment) with parents or other important caregivers? Has he/she developed a sado-masochistic way of relating to his/her current partner? Is the patient controlling and unforthcoming during the course of the interview?

Within the context of object relationships, the mode of relating, i.e. whether the object (person) is considered as a whole object or part object, also needs to be explored. The following example illustrates how a patient has managed to differentiate between the good and bad (part) objects.

Mrs F, a pleasant young woman, sought psychotherapy because she became aware that she needed to develop a long-term, normal relationship with food, a more realistic approach to her depressive feelings and the ability to get on with her life.

She recalled being humiliated and bossed around by both her mother and her sister. She developed an eating disorder in her adolescence as a way of rebelling against her mother's rigidity. She had been married for several years. As she had recently decided to have a baby, she was concerned about her eating difficulty and her capacity to form a relationship with the baby. The assessor wondered whether she was afraid of becoming rigid like her mother and bossing around her own future child. She laughed and warmly responded that she could not possibly reject her mother just because of her bossiness. Despite the resentment of her mother's rigidity (bad part-object), there was still an internalized good enough mother/object. During the assessment, it became quite clear that she was aware of her ambivalent feelings and was concerned not to repeat them with her own future child.

The capacity to sustain at least one meaningful relationship in the past is considered important, as it may help to predict future therapeutic alliance and early termination of treatment (Truant, 1999). Rosenbluth & Yalom (1997) suggest that for those borderline patients where there is an absence of this capacity to sustain at least one meaningful and non-destructive relationship for a year, in-depth psychotherapy should be undertaken with caution. Recent guidelines for the development of services for people suffering from personality disorder indicate that these patients are most appropriately and safely assessed and placed in specialist multidis-ciplinary personality disorder teams preferably within a specialist day patient service (NIMHE, 2003).

Affective capacity

Affects can be broadly described as emotional feeling tones or states (Sandler, 1987), and as signals accompanying an idea, thought or object. They can be considered to constitute the foundations of, or to be reactive to, motivational forces.[1]

Developmentally speaking, affects are the medium of the mother–child interaction. The so-called affective "dialogue" and affective "attunement" (Stern, 1985; Tyson & Tyson, 1990) between mother and baby represent the mortar holding together the build-ing blocks of object relations. As Novey (1961) puts it "Affects are the source of the colour and richness of human experience . . . no human relatedness is conceivable without affective participation."

Ruesh (1948) noted that in some patients, "Verbal, gestural and other symbols are not connected with affect or feelings" and that "Signs used for self-expression originate instead in the somatic sphere". The unimaginative, mundane and circumstantial thought content of psychosomatic patients, described by the French as "Pensée opératoire" (Marty & de M'Uzan, 1963) led Nemiah &

Sifneos (1970) to name a group of patients, who showed a remarkable inability to verbalize their emotional affairs, alexithymic.

Affective capacity refers to the ability to prepare and convey appropriate affective responses (e.g. joy, interest, surprise, anger, shame, fear, anxiety, etc.) to the world in order to communicate and elicit responses from others (Moore & Fine, 1990).

Within the context of assessment, we will be looking for appropriate affects and defensive attempts to ward off affects, linked to memories, images, and thoughts in the past and present.

> Mrs D, an Irish Catholic woman, conveyed with a large grin how she was suffering from mounting depression. She had seemed to take the sudden departure of her husband in her stride, continuing to work obsessively as if nothing had happened. She nursed her second youngest brother who was suffering from AIDS, in addition to weathering her father's recent stroke. She had seen a counsellor for a few sessions, but began to feel more desperate than before.

> During the consultation she revealed, with virtually frozen affect, a wayward and promiscuous way of living in the past, which had led to a number of terminations. She decided to keep one baby, but ten days after the birth of a baby girl, she placed her up for adoption. Soon after, she became severely depressed and took a serious overdose, which left her in coma for a number of days.

> She remarked, without showing any emotions, that ever since this event she has regretted being alive. When the assessor expressed his concern that behind a smiling façade there was enormous pain and a deep sense of hopelessness linking the affect with the memory and the present losses, she started to cry inconsolably. When she stopped crying, she told the assessor how frightened she had been since her suicide attempt of experiencing any feelings for fear of killing herself. When the assessor suggested in-patient admission she was grateful and clearly relieved.

In this case, clarification of the discrepancy between the material presented and affect eventually allowed the patient to acknowledge the underlying seriousness of her condition and how cut-off she had been from her emotional life. In addition, this clinical vignette highlights the presence and importance of defence mechanisms (such as repression, denial, splitting) used as protection against painful affects (guilt, shame).

The use of mechanisms of defence,[2] which can operate singly or in combination, is normal and can have important adaptive functions. These mechanisms actively protect and defend the ego against perceived internal and external dangers such as the loss of object or disapproval. However, such mechanisms can be considered maladaptive or pathological when they are employed rigidly and excessively or when they distort reality. Furthermore, the excessive use of immature and primitive defences such as splitting, rather than more mature ones, such as sublimation, can indicate lesser or greater ego strength.

Frustration tolerance and impulse control

Frustration is a normal human response to any unfulfilled wish, desire, or instinctual demand. The ability to tolerate frustration was considered by Freud (1912) as important in the development of reality testing. The infant realizes during development that certain stimuli can be absent as well as present and that things may come and go. The infant learns that certain stimuli can achieve immediate gratification, while others receive delayed gratification depending on reality.

It is important to assess the patient's capacity to tolerate frustration and delayed gratification. Indeed, there is evidence that the capacity to tolerate frustration is an important indicator for successful psychodynamic psychotherapy. Furthermore, this capacity is associated with pre-mature psychotherapy termination and is related to symptomatic suffering (Frayn, 1992; Wilczek et al., 1998). However, this factor may not be an essential prerequisite for more supportive therapies (Piper et al., 1998).

The manner in which the patient has responded to frustration in the past can serve to guide us as to the level at which he/she may respond in the course of treatment. At one end of the spectrum frustration is worked through without lasting consequences, while at the other extremely poor frustration tolerance can seriously interfere with the limit-setting and boundaries of a therapeutic situation. The latter can therefore lead to extreme impulsive actions such as deliberate self-harm, aggressive or inappropriate sexual behaviour, and/or early drop-out. It is not uncommon for patients to terminate therapy prematurely, or make demands on other professionals after an unexpected or even planned break during therapy.

The mode of presentation, history, and interaction with the assessor can provide useful clues as to whether the patient is able to deal with frustration.

> Mr P, a 34-year-old civil servant, vociferously expressed his frustration at the lack of seats in the waiting area. He elaborated further by describing how he would change the waiting area to allow for better seating arrangements. His frustration and comments were initially considered reasonable by the assessor. As the history unfolded, however, it became clear that Mr P tends to react to any situation that is not to his liking with aggressive outbursts. Moreover, he described that after a break-up of any significant relationship he is unable to contain the turmoil of emotions stirred up in him and reacts by either taking impulsive overdoses or by aggressively pursuing the partner.

Patients, particularly those suffering from emotionally unstable personality disorder, often present with behaviour that is indicative of extremely poor impulse control and low frustration threshold.

Impulse is defined as an application of an internal force to action that is irresistible and has an impelling quality. If thwarted it leads to extreme tension. It is therefore a knee-jerk reaction as opposed to a thoughtful, reflective response. For example, self-harm, substance misuse, and food binges are often impulsive attempts to find a solution in order to deal with painful affects stemming from lack of, or delay in, gratification.

Those patients who present with low frustration tolerance and poor impulse control of a destructive nature are difficult to contain in once-weekly out-patient psychotherapy and may require more specialized settings such as day-patient or residential care.

* * *

To conclude, ego strength, with its components, is a complex concept. There have been a number of studies which have shown a positive relationship between ego strength and treatment outcome (Conte *et al.*, 1991; Kernberg *et al.*, 1972). However, other studies have not found a significant relationship (Luborsky *et al.*, 1980; Weber *et al.*, 1985). Further research is needed in order to identify the significance of ego strength in the psychotherapy process and outcome.

Capacity to form a therapeutic relationship

From a psychodynamic point of view, this capacity is divided into three components, which are simultaneously present (Meissner, 1996):

- the real relationship between the therapist and the patient
- the transference (and counter-transference) relationship
- the therapeutic alliance.

The *real relationship* is the relationship between the patient and the assessor as real people, rather than as working partners or infantile objects in the transference (Freud A., 1954; de Jonghe *et al.*, 1991).

When meeting a patient for the first time, the patient and the assessor are two real people with their own personalities, idiosyncrasies, and mannerisms. These factors may distort the assessment process. The patient may also form an impression of what a psychotherapy journey will be like by using this first encounter as a template.

The origins of the terms transference and counter-transference were referred to earlier. The following definitions, developed by Sandler *et al.* (1992), are more recent and comprehensive. *Transference* is described as

... a specific illusion, which unbeknown to the subject, represents, in some of its aspects, a repetition of a relationship with important figures from the past and is experienced as strictly appropriate to the present and to the particular person involved.

Counter-transference consists instead of "specific emotionally based responses aroused in the analyst by specific qualities of his patients."

The concept of *therapeutic alliance*, or working alliance, has been marked with controversy. Some believe it to be synonymous with transference (Olinick, 1976), while others tend to consider it either as a component of transference (Brenner, 1979; Modell, 1986) or as a completely distinct concept (Meissner, 1992). However, in practice it is difficult at times to make a clear-cut distinction, since the two are in constant interaction and are often interchangeable. Once more Sandler *et al.*'s (1992) clarity comes to our assistance with their definition of therapeutic alliance as

> The patient's conscious or unconscious wish to cooperate and acceptance of the need to deal with internal conflicts with the help of the therapist despite internal or external resistance.

Extensive studies carried out on the therapeutic alliance indicate that a positive therapeutic alliance is the single best predictor of successful outcome in all forms of psychological therapies (DoH, 2001; Orlinsky *et al.*, 1994). There is also some evidence that the capacity to establish a good therapeutic alliance is linked to the therapist's experience and some variables in the patient such as psychological mindedness (Roth & Fonagy, 1996). Furthermore, the personal attributes and culture of both the assessor and the patient contribute to the therapeutic alliance (Ackerman & Hilsenroth, 2001; Shonfeld-Ringel, 2001).

Even though the above considerations may not be especially relevant within the NHS, because the assessor is not usually the treating clinician, it remains of fundamental importance that the patient comes to recognize the existence of internal difficulties that he/she wants to face up to and change. This psychodynamic view of the therapeutic relationship and its subdivisions, however, acquires greater significance during the treatment stage.

The number of assessment consultations needs to be kept to a minimum of one or two, in order to avoid the development of an unnecessary deepening of the relationship (i.e. transference and therapeutic alliance) with the assessor. However, in specific circumstances it can be helpful to undertake an extended assessment (Garelick, 1994; Spurling, 2003). When intensive and extended assessment consultations are required, particularly in emotionally unstable adults and adolescents, it is vital to reach a mutually satisfactory therapeutic decision (Laufer & Laufer, 1984; Rosenbluth & Yalom, 1997).

Concluding remarks

In the preceding two chapters, both generic and specific psycho-dynamic factors have been discussed. In assessing suitability for psychological therapy there are generic factors that are relevant to certainly the most common, if not all, types of psychotherapies. In addition to generic factors (motivation to change and working rela-tionship), some models, hinged on their theory, may also make use of their own specific methods of enquiry in order to determine suit-ability (see, for example, Hawton *et al.*, 1989; Mace, 1995). As previ-ously discussed, psychodynamic psychotherapy relies on specific concepts such as psychological mindedness, ego strength, and capacity to form a therapeutic alliance. However, it appears not only that there is an overlap about what constitute specific charac-teristics for each model, but also that some terms have been misap-propriated or even borrowed from psychodynamic theories (Segal & Blatt, 1993), representing a psychoanalytic drift (Milton, 2001). For example, the therapeutic alliance is clearly a psychodynamic concept that has become part of other treatment modalities.

A trend favoured by some (Holmes & Bateman, 2002) is a rapprochement of different models into a single integrated model. There has been some debate about the so-called brokerage assess-ment, which could be used by psychotherapists of different theo-retical orientations. Although we agree that a brokerage assessment could serve as a useful preliminary tool because it gives a broader view of the patient and allows for reflections on different modali-ties of intervention, we believe that there are major differences in the way different theories formulate or understand a patient.

Notes

1. Affects include drives, stimuli, wishes, needs etc. (Noy, 1982).
2. The definition of the various mechanisms of defence are beyond the scope of this book.

CHAPTER SEVEN

Case formulation

A case formulation is essentially a hypothesis based on the conceptualization and intelligible translation of the individual's central problems. The formulation process should lead to an understanding of the patient in the context of his/her difficulties and it informs as to the most suitable treatment modality.

The referral letter, relevant case notes, information elicited in the interview, and the quality of the interaction during the assessment process pave the way to a descriptive summary of the case. This summary should include history (developmental, family), predisposing, precipitating and perpetuating factors, and diagnosis and risk factors in the context of socio-cultural influences. The collation of this complex and at times even contradictory information to arrive at the formulation in a meaningful and coherent way is not always an easy task. Nevertheless, we are of the opinion that an assessment is not complete without a case formulation. There is evidence that most assessors attempt to reach a formulation in their mind, but that the actual formulation is seldom documented (Perry *et al.*, 1987).

Depending on the assessor's training and theoretical orientation, the formulation may focus principally on unconscious process and conflicts, dysfunctional thoughts and beliefs, or maladaptive learning (Eells, 1997).

A further aim of a formulation is to arrive at a recommendation for treatment, management and, where possible, to predict responses to treatment. These recommendations will include an opinion on suitability and, when appropriate, type of psychological therapy, modality, and length. It may also give indications for drug therapy or offer other alternatives. It is possible to formulate predictions about the patient's vulnerability and risk factors that may hamper psychological therapy.

Moreover, a well thought-out formulation not only provides us with an understanding of the patient's predicament and allows us to make recommendations and predictions, but it is also a helpful training exercise.

Psychodynamic formulation

Following our structured framework, we now deal with the next question to consider.

If the patient is deemed suitable for psychodynamic psychotherapy what is the psychodynamic formulation?

A psychodynamic formulation is a preliminary short description of how the unconscious meaning of the patient's unique difficulties and conflicts is understood. This is achieved by connecting these difficulties with his/her history and the development of his/her internal world, within the context of the interaction between the patient and the assessor. A quotation from Holmes (1991) illustrates this process more poignantly: "Patient and therapist collaboratively act like interpreters of a literary text or musical score trying to grasp the deep structure of the work."

A well thought-out referral letter and previous case notes may already contain elements from which some initial, tentative hypotheses could be formulated. These can be tested, expanded upon, modified, or even rejected during the assessment.

In addition to factors previously mentioned, a psychodynamic formulation will pay special heed to the developmental history, the meaning of symptoms and possible underlying causes, nature of the unconscious conflicts, ego-strength and deficit and quality of object-relations.

Lister *et al.* (1995), in their four-part formulation, consider the following headings:

(i)   summary of the case;
(ii)   discussion of non-dynamic factors;
(iii) psycho-dynamic explanation of central conflicts, object-relations, and defences;
(iv)   prediction of how the patient's dynamics will affect the therapy.

Hinshelwood (1991), on the other hand, acknowledging the work of Menninger (1958) and Malan (1979), emphasizes three areas of object-relationships within a framework that he considers important in reaching a psychodynamic formulation:

(i)   the current life-situation;
(ii)   the infantile object-relations;
(iii) the relationship with the assessor.

Seitz (1966) noted that there was very little consensus between formulations. Since then there have been a number of attempts to specify structured case formulation methods (Horowitz et al., 1989; Luborsky & Crits-Cristoph, 1990; Luborsky *et al.*, 1993) and to improve reliability and validity.

Research, carried out by Malan (1979) in brief psychodynamic psychotherapy, showed that factors considered in a formulation such as good pre-morbid functioning and motivation, clear links between precipitating condition and the meaning of symptomatology, and good response to trial interpretations were all considered good prognostic indicators.

A psychodynamic formulation is also inevitably influenced by the assessor's theoretical background, degree of experience and culture. It is, however, clear that most psychodynamic clinicians share certain basic tenets such as the existence of the unconscious

mental structures, psychic multi-determinism, intra-psychic conflicts, and transference and counter-transference phenomena (Lister
et al., 1995).

This "brief narrative", however, is only a stepping-stone, a plas-
tic procedure, which may well need to be reviewed and modified
in the light of further knowledge of the patient.

The following clinical vignette illustrates how a psychodynamic
formulation can be reached in the course of a psychodynamic
assessment.

History

Ms K, a 24-year-old woman of Middle Eastern origin, went to see her
general practitioner because she was finding it increasingly difficult to
leave her house. Moreover, she could not concentrate on her studies
and was withdrawing from friends. Following a brief assessment, her
GP suggested a course of anxiolytic medication. Due to restriction of
time and the GP's own limitations, he did not take up the seriousness
of her complaints. Ms K returned two weeks later asking to see a
specialist. The letter to the Mental Health Services was brief, indicating
only that she had a phobia about travelling. The psychiatrist, however,
detected an underlying depressive illness and prescribed antidepres-
sive medication, which she was very reluctant to take. He also
acknowledged that there were a number of issues connected with her
past that she was keen to address. The referral letter from the psychiatrist to the assessing psychotherapist highlighted the patient's difficult
relationship with her parents and her eagerness to explore this, as she
believed it affected her other relationships, particularly with men.

Ms K was born and spent her early years in Lebanon until her parents
separated when she was five. Her mother was English and returned to
the UK after the separation. She was brought up by her father until the
age of nine, when he finally decided to send her to a boarding school
in England. He had married twice since then, but she had virtually no
contact with her stepmothers. She maintained a sporadic, and often
angry, contact with her mother and consequently spent the ensuing
years developing a strong sense of independence. However, she often
wondered why her mother had decided to leave her with her father.
Academically she was very successful, and had won a scholarship to a
prestigious university. At the time of the assessment she was studying
for a higher degree in London.

For the previous few months she had found it increasingly difficult to concentrate and was virtually unable to leave her flat. Due to her fear of leaving the flat, her social life became more and more restricted to such an extent that she hardly saw any friends.

Ms K linked the onset of her difficulties to a recent break-up of a six-month long relationship. She admitted that she tended to run away from men who want to commit themselves to her, whereas she pursued those men who showed little interest in her. Most of her relationships had, in fact, been short-lived, and she invariably instigated the break-up. However, it emerged that in the most recent relationship the boyfriend left her without an explanation. Ms K tearfully acknow-ledged the assessor's comment that being left so abruptly had perhaps reminded her of the time she was left by both parents without an adequate explanation. She painfully recounted how lonely she had felt in a foreign country surrounded by strangers. She remembers lying awake in bed longing to be cared for, but at the same time wishing to grow up quickly and be in charge of her own life.

In the course of the assessment she became aware of the degree of her longing for and resentment towards her parents, who did not provide her with a loving and secure home. She believes that her disrupted childhood, in which she felt shuttled from one parent to another before finally being left in a boarding school to fend for herself, had made it very difficult for her to trust anyone in a relationship. Although she longed to be in a loving relationship and have a family, as soon as someone showed her affection she became cold and distant.

After her initial reticence, which conveyed her defensive armour, the assessor was able to make contact with the frightened little girl part of her who was desperate to be heard and understood. This emotional contact made the assessor aware of how easily "rescue fantasies" could be triggered in anyone who would try to get close to her.

Formulation

Eventually the assessor reached the following psychodynamic formulation.

Ms K, a 24-year-old single woman suffering from phobic-anxiety, was referred by her general practitioner to the psychiatrist, who detected an underlying depressive disorder.

She was brought up in Lebanon by her English mother and Lebanese father until the age of five. Her mother left her in the care of her father and returned to England. Her father, who remarried several times, could not cope with her and sent her to boarding school abroad. Ms K felt unloved and abandoned by both parents, with whom she maintains a distant relationship. She developed a fierce sense of independence as a way of coping with her thwarted dependency needs. Her need to terminate relationships after a short time could be understood as a manifestation of her need to be cruelly in control, while unconsciously repeating what was done to her by her parents. Until the recent break-up, Ms K was unaware of any difficulties. In fact she had been academically successful and enjoyed a good social life. The unresolved conflicts of the past and her ambivalence towards her parents had, however, resurfaced after the recent abandonment. Furthermore, her travelling phobia and withdrawal could be explained as her way of defending herself against fear of losing control as well as expressing the unconscious need to be looked after.

Ms K was well motivated, guardedly open to self-reflection and willing to engage, in order to make sense of her pattern of behaviour, rather than be symptomatically treated for her problems with medication only.

The history reveals a moderate depressive illness with marked phobic anxiety behaviour. There is no previous psychiatric history or any history of self-harm. There seems to have been some good nurturing in her early years, which allowed her to develop a degree of inner strength. By contrast her difficulty in forming long-term relationships indicates a degree of ego-weakness. Splitting, denial, identification with the aggressor, and reaction formation were the prominent defence mechanisms used by Ms K.

A course of psychodynamic psychotherapy was recommended with some cautionary notes. In view of Ms K's conflicts regarding abandonment, there was a possibility of her dropping out of therapy prematurely. There was also a strong likelihood that "rescue and parenting fantasies" may be evoked in the transference relationship. As there have been abandonment issues, the stability of the setting and the provision of a reasonably lengthy therapeutic contract with the same therapist need to be carefully considered.

This clinical vignette illustrates the process of understanding this particular patient in the context of her difficulties, leading to the most suitable treatment modality with cautionary notes. We have enlarged on purpose the psychodynamic formulation in order to clarify some relevant points. In practice, however, a psychodynamic formulation should be brief and to the point and include the following:

- a very brief summary of the case
- a psychodynamic understanding including defences and developmental issues
- recommendations for treatment
- prognostic implications.

CHAPTER EIGHT

Post-assessment routes

I n the previous chapters we concentrated on the referral process and the various stages of assessment that led to a comprehensive psychodynamic formulation. The formulation helps to sketch an articulated picture of the unique world of the patient and guides the patient and the assessor to a mutual, appropriate, and agreed plan of action.

In certain circumstances, however, the assessment might provide helpful and important insight into issues that the patient may be able to deal with without further need for psychotherapy. Recommendations for no psychological treatment are just as important as recommendations for treatment.

What treatment modality, where and by whom can the patient best be helped?

Post-assessment options

The assessor, in his/her formulation, needs to reach a decision regarding the most suitable form of management. A number of patients may not benefit from a psychological intervention not just because of their lack of motivation and unwillingness to commit to a working relationship, but also because of florid psychotic episodes, continuous substance-related disorders, and organic mental conditions. The assessor should then discuss and explain the reasons why psychological therapy is not appropriate. He/she should also discuss alternatives that might be more appropriate and helpful. These may include, for example, referral to a psychiatrist, day hospital, CMHTs, specialist services.

In very few cases, the assessment process seems to be sufficient and no further action is needed. In other cases, the timing may not be right and patients may return with increased motivation and prepared to commit themselves.

When the outcome of the assessment indicates that the patient is suitable for a psychological therapy, the assessor needs to make a decision on the most suitable modality of treatment. The assessor needs to give an explanation of treatment modalities locally available (these may be counselling, cognitive-behavioural, psychodynamic, systemic, and integrative). A more detailed explanation including the pros and cons of the various modalities is then given to the patient. It is important that the patient fully understands the implications of such commitment and has grasped the information given by the assessor, so as to be in a position to make an informed choice. The predilection of the patient for one type of therapy over another and his/her choice of therapist may need to be taken into consideration.

If the assessor reaches the conclusion that not only is the patient suitable for psychotherapy but psychodynamic psychotherapy would provide the most appropriate treatment modality of choice, the following options may be considered and discussed:

- individual (brief-focal, intermediate, and long-term)
- group
- couples
- family.

With regard to treatment length, for individual therapy it is generally assumed that brief-focal is up to six months, intermediate is twelve to eighteen months, and long-term is two years or more. The length of time for group psychotherapy is a minimum of eighteen months. The length of treatment time for couples and families varies.

In some cases patients may be deemed suitable for psycho-dynamic psychotherapy, but require more intensive and prolonged psychotherapy, which the local resources are unable to accommo-date. The assessor needs to be informed about other options such as psychotherapy organizations offering reduced-fee schemes, local private practices, and the voluntary sector.

In addition to the most suitable modality of treatment, where possible, the assessor needs to consider the best match between that particular patient and a prospective therapist.

Although some preliminary findings demonstrate that the personality match of patient and therapist can affect treatment outcome (Kantrowitz *et al.*, 1990), there is as yet no substantial evidence to support this (DoH, 2001).

As the waiting time between assessment and treatment may vary in length depending on the availability of resources, many specialist services offer the possibility of reviewing the patient's situation from time to time while he/she remains on the waiting list.

Finally, the assessor will be in the position to write back to the referrer. The letter should be succinct and to the point, outlining the patient's complaints and their meanings, his/her understanding of the development of such difficulties, and a formulation containing the assessor's hypothesis and recommendations for management and, where possible, some prognostic indicators.

Availability of resources

As we said earlier, the availability of resources needs to be taken into consideration when recommending psychological therapies, since they may influence the selection of and subsequent allocation to different modalities and therapists.

Psychotherapy services, like the majority of specialities within the NHS, are faced with numerous challenges. Efficiency, equity, level of expertise, and training, funding, accessibility, and research facilities constitute just a few of these issues.

Although it is now well recognized and, indeed, recommended (Parry & Richardson, 1996) that the various types of psychotherapy should be widely available across mental health services and considered as a matter of course, this has not been matched by an adequate increase in funding for this recommended expansion.

As proposed in our introduction, the process of assessment exemplifies these very issues and the important initial contact with a specialist service can therefore be skewed by the availability of resources.

Patients come for help with their own preferences and expectations, which can be at variance with what the service is able to provide. For example, they may ask for a therapist of their own sex, for someone who is knowledgeable about their specific concerns or their culture and language, or who can be available outside of working hours. Equally, the assessor may have difficulty in providing the appropriate type of therapeutic modality for a particular patient, matching him/her with an appropriate therapist, or offering the most suitable length of therapy.

Furthermore, there are a number of other important constraints, which are often overlooked, such as: availability of rooms, transport and parking restrictions, crèche facilities, and changes in patients' circumstances.

Striving for a better service, we always try our best to meet as many of these needs as possible. Many services are now more accessible, better coordinated and more user-friendly, and offer a range of psychological therapies. However, it is an unfortunate reality that at times the most difficult patients may end up being seen by the least experienced member of the team. Some cases may not receive adequate or sufficiently intensive treatment, and others may be lost while waiting.

CHAPTER NINE

Concluding remarks

The aim of this work is to highlight the role of assessment within psychological therapies with a special reference to the psychodynamic approach.

We have explored how the various nuances of the first encounter may shape attitudes and expectations in both the patient and the assessor/doctor. This initial encounter is a joint enterprise where unrealistic expectations are challenged and concerns are empathically listened to and addressed with sensitivity without undermining the patient's capacity to make decisions. Mutual thinking about the difficulties, reaching an understanding, and imparting information allows the patient to reflect and make appropriate choices.

We have attempted to examine the subtle interaction between two "strangers" by paying attention to verbal and non-verbal communication cues. With the help of clinical vignettes we examined in detail how the patient's presentation and narrative may assist the assessor gradually to arrive at a provisional diagnosis and a psychodynamic formulation.

We have traced the various steps of the assessment procedure from the pre-referral process to the psychodynamic formulation and recommendations, and also emphasized how training, experience, research knowledge, and familiarity with existing mental health services are essential prerequisites for any assessor in the NHS.

We stress the importance of considering with the patient a number of psychological treatment modalities, of which the psychodynamic approach is just one of many. An explanation of the various treatment modalities available within the service will allow the patient to reach a more informed choice. Furthermore, we highlight the inevitable consequences of the limited resources.

In the current atmosphere of incessant scrutiny of the NHS, the continual changes are often not in keeping with the reality of its workforce. Although psychological therapy should now be considered as a matter of course for all patients suffering from mental health problems, and we emphasize the importance of patient choice, which may be fuelled by unrealistic promises on the part of the government, the reality often fails to tally with the expectations. Hence, the need to maintain good practice, professional skills, and a clear focus becomes even more paramount.

We offer this work hoping that we have succeeded in our aims of presenting some of the existing literature and research evidence in a synthesized form and providing a framework for the formalized teaching of assessment, particularly in psychodynamic psychotherapy. Finally, we hope that this work will provoke further thought and debate on issues connected with assessment.

Dear

Dr _____ has asked us to see you concerning your difficulties and with a view to discussing your future treatment. We would be grateful if you would contact my Secretary on _____ (at times there is an answer phone) on receipt of this letter to confirm that you wish to be offered an appointment.
Looking forward to hearing from you.

Yours sincerely

APPENDIX TWO
Letter to be sent out with questionnaire

Dear

I write to offer you an appointment for an assessment for psychotherapy on _____ in the _____
This interview should take between one and one and a half hours and will provide us with the opportunity of discussing together your present difficulties and possibilities for further treatment.

Please complete the attached form and return it to me, in the pre-paid envelope enclosed, by _____ to let me know if it is convenient for you to attend. As you will understand, we have a waiting list for appointments so if I have not received confirmation from you by this date I must assume that you no longer wish to proceed with psychotherapy and we will then offer this appointment to another patient.

It would be extremely helpful if you could fill in the enclosed standard questionnaire and return it with the form. If you feel you may have difficulty in completing this, you can bring it with you to your appointment and any queries you have can then be discussed.

Yours sincerely

Enc
N.B. Please note that there is very limited parking near the _____ Please take this into account and try to arrive on time.

Questionnaire

QUESTIONNAIRE

Confidential

When you come for your preliminary interview you will have the opportunity to discuss your difficulties with me and this is of course the most important way of understanding them. However, it can be helpful for both of us if you are able to fill in this confidential questionnaire and return it to me before you come, although this is not obligatory.

The questionnaire begins with more factual information, while the later questions are of a more subjective nature. It can be helpful to read all the questions first, although you are of course free to answer them in any order.

Name _____

Date of Birth_____

Address _____

_____

Telephone _____

Date   _____

Name and address of your GP _____

_____

_____

1   Could you please fill in some details about your family?

	Age now or at death	If dead, your own age when he/she died	Occupation
Father:			
Mother:			
Brothers & sisters: Names			
Spouse/ Partner:			
Children: Names			

2   Could you tell us about your schooling and further education?

3   Please tell us about your past employment, including your
    present job.

AGE		Employment	Reason for leaving
From	To		

4   Have you had any psychological help in the past? If so,
    could you please let us know the following details?

   (1)   *In-patient or day-patient treatment*
         Name of hospital   Approx. length of stay   Year

   (2)   *Out-patient treatment*
         Name of hospital   Approx. duration or   Year
                                   number of visits

   (3)   *Previous psychotherapy*
         Name of hospital   Approx. duration   Year
                                   and therapist and
                                   type of therapy

5   Have you ever tried to harm yourself or made a suicide attempt?

Have you ever been in trouble with the law?

Could you tell us something about your use of alcohol and drugs in the past and now?

6   Could you please give us a brief description of your difficulties as you see them, mentioning how long you had them, including your present condition?

In what way do your difficulties affect your everyday life?

What aspects of your life do you enjoy the most?

7   Do you think you could tell us a little more about your family, including the general atmosphere at home and in particular any major changes during your childhood, including separations from the family?

8   If you have a partner and/or children do you have any difficulties in your relationship with your partner or members of your family?

Do you have any sexual problems or difficulty in your sexual relationships? If so, try to describe them.

What are your present domestic circumstances? Are they difficult in any way?

9   Please mention any difficulties or satisfactions in your working life, including your plans for the future.

10   What form of treatment do you expect and in what way do you think it might help you?

Please use this space if there is any other relevant or helpful information relating to your present difficulties (or to expand on any of the earlier questions).

APPENDIX FOUR

Name _____

Address _____

_____

_____

Telephone Number _____

*I can/cannot attend my appointment on _____

*I no longer wish to be considered for psychotherapy

As cancellations do occasionally occur, please indicate whether you would be able to attend an appointment at short notice.

*I would/would not be able to attend an appointment at short notice

Contact telephone number (if different from above) _____

Signature _____

Date _____

*Please delete as applicable

REFERENCES

Ackerman, S. J., & Hilsenroth, M. J. (2001). A review of therapist characteristics and techniques negatively impacting the therapeutic alliance. *Psychotherapy, 38*(2): 171–185.

Appelbaum, A. (1972). A critical re-examination of the concept "Motivation for change" in psychoanalytical treatment. *International Journal of Psychoanalysis, 53*: 51–59.

Appelbaum, S. (1973). Psychological-mindedness: word, concept and essence. *International Journal of Psycho-analysis, 54*: 35–46.

Bateman, A. (2000). Personal communication.

Bergin, A. & Garfield, S. (1994). *Handbook of Psychotherapy and Behavior Change.* New York: John Wiley and Sons.

Bernal, G., Bonilla, J., Padilla-Cotto, L., & Perez-Prado, E. M. (1998). Factors associated to outcome in psychotherapy: an effectiveness study in Puerto Rico. *Journal of Clinical Psychology, 54*: 329–342.

Bhugra, D., & Burns, A. (Eds.) (1995). *Management forPsychiatrists.* London: Gaskell.

British Medical Journal (2000). Editor's Choice: The gap between expectations and reality. *320*: 1345.

Bowlby, J. (1988). *A Secure Base: Parent–Child Attachment and Healthy Human Development.* New York: Basic Books.

Brenner, C. (1979). Working alliance, therapeutic alliance and transference. *Journal of the American Psychoanalytic Association, 27*: 137–157.

Brown, T., & Barlow, D. (1992). Co-morbidity among anxiety disorders: implications for treatment and *DSM-IV*. *Journal of Consulting and Clinical Psychol*ogy, *60*: 835–844.

Busch, F. (1986. The occasional question in psychoanalytical assessments. *International Review of Psychoanalysis, 13*: 453–461.

Campbell, P., & Russell, G. (1983). The assessment of neurotic and personality disorders in adults. In: G. Russell & L. A. Hersov (Eds.) *The Neurosis and Personality Disorders. Handbook of Psychiatry.* Cambridge: Cambridge University Press.

Caparrotta, L. (1997). The problem of urgency in adolescence (unpublished paper).

Caparrotta, L. (2000). Personal communication.

Coker, S., Vize, C., Wade, T., & Cooper, P. J. (1993). Patients with bulimia nervosa who fail in cognitive behaviour therapy. *International Journal of Eating Disorders, 13*: 35–40.

Coltart, N. (1986). Diagnosis and assessment of suitability for psychoanalytic psychotherapy. *Contemporary Psychoanalysis , 22*(4): 560–569.

Coltart, N. (1988). The assessment of psychological-mindedness in the diagnostic interview. *British Journal of Psychiatry, 153*: 819–820.

Conte, H., & Ratto, R. (1997). Self-report measure of psychological mindedeness. In: M. McCallum & W. E. Piper (Eds.), *Psychological Mindedness: A Contemporary Understanding* (pp. 12–21). Mahwah, NJ: Lawrence Erlbaum.

Conte, H., Plutchik, R., Picard, S., & Karasu, T. (1991). Can personality traits predict psychotherapy outcome? *Comprehensive Psychiatry, 32*: 66–72.

Cooper, J., & Alfillé, H. (Eds.) (1998). *Assessment in Psychotherapy.* London: Karnac Books.

Davies, S. (2003). Personal communication.

Deane, F. (1993). Attendance and drop out from outpatient psychotherapy in New Zealand. *Community & Mental Health New Zealand, 6*(1): 34–51.

De Jonghe, F., Rijnierse, P., & Janssen, R. (1991). Aspects of the analytic relationship. *International Journal of Psychoanalysis, 72*: 693–707.

Department of Health (DoH) (2001). *Treatment Choice in Psychological Therapies and Counselling.* London: DoH Publications, 23044.

Diagnostic and Statistical Manual of Mental Disorders (DSM-IV) (4th edn) (1994) Washington, DC: American Psychiatric Association.

Diatkine, R. (1968). Indications and contraindications for psychoanalytic treatment. *International Journal of Psychoanalysis, 49*: 266–270.

Eells, T. D. (Ed.) (1997). *Handbook of Psychotherapy Case Formulation*. London: Guildford Press.

Feld, R., Woodside, B. W., Kaplan, A. S., Olmsted, M. P., & Carter, C. (2001). Pre-treatment motivational enhancement therapy for eating disorders: a pilot study. *International Journal of Eating Disorders, 9*(4): 393–400.

Fonagy, P., Leigh, T., Steele, M., Steele, H., Kennedy, R. Mattoon, G., Margeet, M., & Gerber, A. (1996). The relation of attachment status, psychiatric classification, and response to psychotherapy. *Journal of Consulting and Clinical Psychology, 64*: 22–31.

Frayn, D. H. (1992). Assessment factors associated with pre-mature psychotherapy termination. *American Journal of Psychotherapy, 46*(2): 250–261.

Freud, A. (1954). The widening scope of indications for psycho-analysis. *Journal of the American Psychoanalytical Association, 2*: 607–620.

Freud, S. (1893–1895). Studies on hysteria. *S.E., II*: 301–302. London: Hogarth.

Freud, S. (1905). On psychotherapy. *S. E., VII*: 257–268. London: Hogarth.

Freud, S. (1912). Types of onset of neurosis. *S. E., XII*: 227. London: Hogarth.

Gabbard, G. (2000). *Psychodynamic Psychiatry*. Washington, DC: American Psychiatric Press.

Garelick, A. (1994). Psychotherapy assessment: theory and practice. *Psychoanalytical Psychotherapy, 8*(2): 101–116.

Garelick, A. (1998). Reflections on purchasing psychotherapy services: the importance of unconscious factors. *Psychoanalytical Psychotherapy, 12*: 103–110.

Garfield, S. L. (1994). Research on client variables in psychotherapy. In: A. Bergin & S. L. Garfield (Eds.), *Handbook of Psychotherapy and Behavior Change*. (4th edn) (pp. 72–113). New York: John Wiley & Sons.

Gelder, M., & Lopez-Llbor, J. (2000) *The New Oxford Textbook of Psychiatry*. Oxford University Press.

General Medical Council (2001). *Good Medical Practice* (3rd edn), London.

Ghaffari, K. (2000). Personal communication.

Goldberg, A. (1994). Farewell to the Objective Analyst. *International Journal of Psycho-analysis, 75*: 21–30.

Gozzetti, G., & Sava, V. (2001). La nascita della psicosi in adolescenza. Paper presented at the Italian Congress of Psychiatry, Cosenza.

Hartmann, H. (1958). *Ego Psychology and the Problem of Adaptation*. New York: International Universities Press.

Hawton, K., Salkovskis, P. M., Kirk, J., & Clark, D. M. (1989). *Cognitive Behaviour Therapy forPsychiatric Problems. A Practical Guide*. Oxford University Press.

Hinshelwood, R. (1991). Psychodynamic formulation in assessment for psychotherapy. *British Journal of Psychotherapy, 8*(2): 166–174.

Høglend, P. (1996). Motivation for brief dynamic psychotherapy. *Psychotherapy and Psychosomatics, 65*: 209–215.

Høglend, P., Sørlie, T., Sørbie, O., Heyerdahl, O., & Amlo, S. (1992). Long-term changes after brief dynamic psychotherapy: symptomatic versus dynamic assessment. *Acta Psychiatrica Scandinavica, 86*: 165–172.

Høglend, P., Sørlie, T., Heyerdahl, O., Sørbie, O., & Amlo, S. (1993). Brief dynamic psychotherapy: patient suitability treatment length and outcome. *Journal of Psychotherapy Practice and Research*, 2: 230–241.

Høglend, P., Engelstad, V., Sørbie, Ø., Heyerdahl, O., & Amlo, S. (1994). The role of insight in exploratory psychodynamic psychotherapy. *British Journal of Medical Psychology, 67*: 305–317.

Holmes, J. (Ed.) (1991). *Textbook of Psychotherapy in Psychiatric Practice*. London: Churchill Livingstone.

Holmes, J. (2002). All you need is cognitive behaviour therapy? *British Medical Journal, 324*: 288–294.

Holmes, J., & Bateman, A. (2002). *Psychotherapy Integration: Models and Methods*. Oxford: Oxford University Press.

Horowitz, M. J., Marmar, C., Weiss, D. S., De Witt, K. N., & Rosenbaum, R. (1984). Brief psychotherapy of bereavement reactions: the relationship of process to outcome. *Archives of General Psychiatry, 41*: 438–448.

Huws, R. (1992). Non-attendances at a marital and sexual difficulties clinic: a controlled intervention study. *International Journal of Social Psychiatry, 38*(4): 304–308.

International Classification of Diseases (ICD-10) (1992). *Classification of Mental and Behavioural Disorders* (10th edn). Geneva: World Health Organization.

Jenkins, G. R., Hale, R., Pappanastassiou, M., Crawford, M., & Tyrer, P. (2002). Suicide rate 22 years after parasuicide: cohort study. *British Medical Journal, 325*: 1155.

Kakar, S. (1985). Psychoanalysis and non-western cultures. *International Review of Psychoanalysis, 12*: 441–448.

Kantrowitz, J. L., Katz, A. L., & Paolitto, F. (1990). Follow-up of psychoanalysis five to ten years after termination: III. The relation between the resolution of the transference and the patient–analyst match. *Journal of the American Psychoanalytic Association*, 38: 655–678.

Kazdin, A., Mazurick, J. L., & Bass, D. (1993). Risk for attrition in treatment of antisocial children and families. *Journal of Clinical Child Psychology*, 22: 2–16.

Keithly, L., Samples, S. J., & Strupp, H. H. (1980). Patient motivation as a predictor as process and outcome in psychotherapy. *Psychotherapy & Psychosomatics*, 33: 87–97.

Kernberg, O., Burstein, E., Coyne, L., Appelbaum, A., Horowitz, L., & Voth, H. (1972). Psychotherapy and psychoanalysis: final report of the Menninger Foundation's psychotherapy research. *Bulletin of the Menninger Clinic*, 36: 1–275.

Killaspy, H., Bannerjee, S., King, M., & Lloyd, M. (2000). Prospective controlled study of psychiatric outpatient non-attendance. *British Journal of Psychoanalysis*, 176: 160–165.

Klauber, J. (1986). *Difficulties in the Analytic Encounter*. London: Free Association.

Knud, J. (1999). Editorial. *Acta Psychiatrica Scandinavica*, 99: 85–86.

Kohut, H. (1996). *The Chicago Institute Lectures*. P. Tolpin & M. Tolpin (Eds.). New York: The Analytic Press.

Laing, R. D., (1967). *The Politics of Experience*. New York: Pantheon.

Lambert, M. J., & Anderson, E. M. (1996). Assessment for the time limited psychotherapies. In: L. J. Dickstein, M. B. Riba, & J. M. Oldham (Eds.), *Review of Psychiatry* (pp. 23–42). Washington, DC: APA.

Laufer, M., & Laufer, E. (1984). *Adolescence and Developmental Breakdown. A Psychoanalytic View*. New Haven: Yale University Press.

Limentani, A. (1972). The assessment of analysability: a major hazard in selection for psychoanalysis. *International Journal of Psycho-analysis*, 53: 357–361.

Lister, E., Auchincloss, E., & Cooper, A. (1995). The psychodynamic formulation. In: H. Schwartz, E. Bleiberg, & S. H. Weissman (Eds.), *Psychodynamic Concepts in General Psychiatry*. Washington, DC: American Psychiatric Press.

Loumidis, K., & Shropshire, J. (1997). Effect of waiting time on appointment attendance with clinical psychologists and length of treatment. *Irish Journal of Psychological Medicine*, 14(2): 49–54.

Luborsky, L., & Crits-Cristoph, P. (Eds.) (1990). *Understanding Transference: The CCRT Method*. New York: Basic Books.

Luborsky, L., Mintz, J., Auerbach, A., Crits-Cristoph, P., Bachrach, H., Todd, T., Johnson, M., Cohen, M., & O'Brien, C. (1980). Predicting the outcome of psychotherapy: findings of the Penn Psychotherapy Project. *Archives of General Psychiatry, 37*: 471–481.

Luborsky, L., Crits-Christoph, P., Mintz, J., & Auerbach, A. (1988). *Who Will Benefit from Psychotherapy? Predicting Therapeutic Outcomes.* New York: Basic Books.

Luborsky, L., Barber, J., Binder, J., Curtis, J., Dahl, H., Horowitz, L., Perry, C., Schacht, T., Sibershatz, G., & Teller, V. (1993). Transference-related measures: a new class Based on psychotherapy sessions. In: N. E. Miller, L. Luborsky, J. Barber, & J. Docherty (Eds.), *Psychodynamic Treatment Research: A Handbook for Clinical Practice*, (pp. 326–341). New York: Basic Books.

Mace, C. (Ed.) (1995). *The Art and Science of Assessment in Psychotherapy.* New York: Routledge.

Malan, D. H. (1979). *Individual Psychotherapy and the Science of Psychodynamics.* London: Butterworths.

Marcus Aurelius (161–180 AD) (2000). The nature of change. In: M. Forstater (Ed.), *The Spiritual Teachings of Marcus Aurelius.* London: Hodder & Stoughton.

Marty, P., & de M'Uzan, M. (1963). La "pensée opératoire". *Revue de Français de Psychoanalis, 27* (Suppl.): 1345.

McCabe, R., Heath, C., Burns, T., & Priebe, S. (2002). Engagement of patients with psychosis in the consultation: conversation analytic study. *British Medical Journal, 325*: 1148–1151.

McCallum, M., & Piper, W. E. (1990). A controlled study of effectiveness and patient suitability for short term group psychotherapy. *International Journal of.Group Psychotherapy, 40*: 431–452.

McCallum, M., & Piper, W. E. (1997). *Psychological Mindedness: A Contemporary Understanding.* Mahwah, NJ: Lawrence Erlbaum.

McCallum, M., Piper, W., Ogrodniczuk, J., & Joyce, A. (2003). Relationships among psychological mindedness, alexithymia and outcome in four forms of short-term psychotherapy. *Psychology & Psychotherapy: Theory, Research and Practice, 76*: 133–144.

Meissner, S. J. (1992). The concept of therapeutice alliance. *Journal of the American Psychoanalytic Association, 40*: 1059–1087.

Meissner, S. J. (1996). *The Therapeutic Alliance.* New Haven: Yale University Press.

Menninger, K. (1958). *Theory of Psychoanalytic Technique.* London: Imago.

Meyer, B., Pilkonis, P., Proietti, J., Heape, C., & Egan, M. (2001). Attachment styles and personality disorders as predictors of symptom course. *Journal of Personality Disorders, 15*: 371–389.

Meyer, B., Pilkonis, P., Krupnickl, J., Egan, M., Simmens, S., & Sotsky, S. (2002). Treatment expectancies, patient alliance and outcome: further analyses from the NIMH treatment of depression collaborative research programme. *Journal of Consulting and Clinical Psychology, 70*: 1051–1055.

Miller, N., Luborsky, L., Barber, J., & Docherty, J. (1993). *Psychodynamic Treatment Research: A Handbook for Clinical Practice.* New York: Basic Books.

Miller, W. R., Benefield, G., & Tonigan, J. (1993). Enhancing motivation for change in problem drinking: a controlled comparison of two therapist styles. *Journal of Consulting and Clinical Psychology, 61*(3): 455–461.

Milton, J. (1997). Why assess? Psychoanalytical assessment in the NHS. *Psychoanalytical Psychotherapy, 11*(1): 47–58.

Milton, J. (2001). Psychoanalysis and cognitive behaviour therapy—rival paradigms or common grounds? *International Journal of Psychoanalysis, 82*: 431–447.

Modell, A. H. (1986). The missing element in Kohut's cure. *Psychoanalytic Inquiry, 6*: 367–385.

Moore, B., & Fine, B. (1990). *Psychoanalytic Terms & Concepts.* The American Psychoanalytic Association. New Haven: Yale University Press.

National Institute of Mental Health (Executive) (NIMH(E)) (2003). *Personality Disorder: No Longer a Diagnosis of Exclusion.* London: Department of Health Publications, 30502.

Nemiah, J. C., & Sifneos, P. E. (1970). Affect and fantasy in patients with psychosomatic disorders. In: O. W. Hill (Ed.), *Modern Trends in Psychosomatic Medicine,* Volume 2 (pp. 26–34). London: Butterworth.

NHS Executive (2000). *Psychological Therapies—Working in Partnership.* London: Department of Health Publications.

Nicholson, I. (1994). Factors involved in failure to keep initial appointments with mental health professionals. *Hospital & Community Psychiatry, 45*: 276–278.

Novey, S. (1961). Further considerations on affect theory in psychoanalysis. *International Journal of Psycho-analysis, 42*: 21–31.

Noy, P. (1982). A revision of the psychoanalytic theory of affect. *Annals of Psychoanalysis, 10*: 139–186.

Olinick, S. L. (1976). Parallel analysing functions in working ego and observing ego: the treatment alliance. *Journal of Philadelphia Association of Psychoanalysis, 3*: 3–21.

Orlinsky, D. E., Grawe, K., & Parks, B. (1994). Process and outcome in psychotherapy. In: A. Bergin & S. Garfield (Eds.), *Handbook of Psychotherapy and Behaviour Change* (4th edn) (pp. 270–376). New York: John Wiley and Sons.

Orlinsky, D., Rønnested, M., & Willutzki, U. (2004). Fifty years of psychotherapy process outcome research: continuity and change. In: *Bergin and Garfield's Handbook of Psychotherapy and Behavior Change* (5th edn) (pp. 307–389). New York: John Wiley and Sons.

Parry, G., & Richardson, A. (1996). *NHS Psychotherapy Services in England: Review of Strategic Policy*. London: Department of Health.

Partridge, E. (1966). *Origins: A Short Etymological Dictionary of Modern English*. London & Henly: Routledge & Kegan Paul.

Pazzagli, A., & Rossi Monti, M. (1999). Psicoanalisi e diagnosi psichiatrica. In: G. Berti Ceroni & A. Correale (Eds.), *Psicoanalisi e Psichiatria* (pp. 43–59). Milan: Raffaello Cortina.

Perry, S., Cooper, A., & Michels, R. (1987). The psychodynamic formulation: its purpose, structure and clinical applications. *American Journal of Psychiatry, 144*: 543–550.

Pine, F. (1990). *Drive, Ego, Object, and Self: A Synthesis for Clinical Work*. New York: Basic Books.

Piper, W. E., Joyce, A., Azim, H., & Rosie, J. (1994). Patient characteristics and success in day treatment. *Journal of Nervous & Mental Distress, 182*: 381–386.

Piper, W. E., Joyce, A., McCallum, M., & Azim, H. (1998). Interpretive and supportive forms of psychotherapy and patient personality variables. *Journal of Consulting and Clinical Psychology, 66*: 558–567.

Richardson, P. (1997). ABC of mental health: psychological treatments. *British Medical Journal, 315*: 733–735.

Richardson, P. (2001). Evidence-based practice and psychodynamic psychotherapies. In: C. Mace, S. Moorey, & B. Roberts (Eds.), *Evidence in the Psychological Therapies* (pp. 157–173). London: Routledge.

Rosenbaum, B., Selzer, M. A., Velbak, K., Hougaard, E., & Sommerlund, B. (1997). The Dynamic Assessment Interview: testing the psychodynamic assessment variables. *Acta Psychiatrica Scandinavica, 95*: 531–538.

Rosenbaum, R. L., & Horowitz, M. J. (1983). Motivation for psycho-therapy: a factorial and conceptual analysis. *Psychotherapy Theory and Research: Practical Training, 20*: 346–354.

Rosenbluth, M., & Yalom, I. D. (Eds.) (1997). *Treating Difficult Personality Disorders*. San Francisco: Jossey-Bass.

Ross, H., & Hardy, G. (1999). GP referrals to adult psychological services: a research agenda for promoting needs-led practice through the involvement of mental health clinicians. *British Journal of Medical Psychology, 72*: 75–91.

Roter, D. L. , Hall, J., Kern, D., Barker, R., Cole, K., & Roca, R. (1995). Improving physicians' interviewing skills and reducing patients' emotional distress: a randomized clinical trial. *Archive of Internal Medicine, 155*: 1877–1884.

Roth, A., & Fonagy, P. (1996). *What Works for Whom?* New York: Guildford Press.

Royal College of Psychiatrists (2002). Vulnerable patients, vulnerable doctors. Good practice in our clinical relationships. Council Report CR101.

Ruesh, J. (1948). The infantile personality: the core problem of psycho-somatic medicine. *Psychosomatic Medicine, 10*: 134–143.

Runeson, B. S. (2002). Suicide after parasuicide. *British Medical Journal, 325*: 1125–1126.

Sackett, D., Rosenberg, W., Gray, J., Haynes, R., & Richardson, W. (1996). Evidence-based medicine: what it is and what it is not (Editorial). *British Medical Journal, 312*: 71–72

Salomon, S., Gerrity, E., & Muff, A. (1992). Efficacy of treatments for post-traumatic stress disorder. An empirical review. *Journal of the American Medical Association, 268*: 633–638.

Sandler, J. (1987). The role of affects in psychoanalytic theory. In: J. Sandler (Ed.), *From Safety to Superego* (pp. 285–297). London: Karnac.

Sandler, J., & Dreher, A. U. (1996). *What Do Psychoanalysts Want?* The New Library of Psychoanalysis. London: Routledge.

Sandler, J., Dare, C., & Holder, A. (1992). *The Patient and the Analyst*. London: Karnac .

Schachter, J. (1997). Transference and counter-transference dynamics in the assessment process. *Psychoanalytical Psychotherapy, 11*(1): 59–71.

Schafer, R. (1970). The psychoanalytic vision of reality. *International Journal of Psycho-analysis, 51*: 279–297.

Schulte-Markwort, M., Romer, G., Behenish, A., Bilke, O., Fegert, J., & Knolker, U. (1999). Werkstattberich der Arbeitsgruppe Achse I:

92   REFERENCES

Sujektive Dimensionen, Ressourcen und Behandlungsvorausst-zungen. *Prax. Kinderpsychol. Kinderpsych.*, *48*(8): 589–601.

Sedlak, V. (1989). Disavowal and assessment for psychotherapy. *Psychoanalytical Psychotherapy*, 4: 97–107.

Segal, Z. V., & Blatt, S. J. (Eds.) (1993). *The Self in Emotional Distress: Cognitive and Psychodynamic Perspectives*. New York: Guildford Press.

Seitz, P.F. (1966). The consensus problem in psychoanalytic research. In: L. Gottschalk & L. Auerbach (Eds.), *Methods of Research and Psychotherapy* (pp. 209–225). New York: Appleton-Century-Crofts.

Sennett, R. (1998). *The Corrosion of Character*. New York: WW Norton.

Shapiro, D., Barkham, M., Rees, A., Hardy, G., Reynold, S., & Startup, M. (1994). Effects of treatment duration and severity of depression on the effectiveness of cognitive-behavioural and psychodynamic-interpersonal psychotherapy. *Journal of Consulting Clinical Psychology*, *62*: 522–534.

Sharp, D. J., & Hamilton, W. (2001). Non-attendance at general practices and outpatient clinics. *British Medical Journal*, *323*: 1081–1082.

Shill, M. A., & Lumley, M. A. (2002). The psychological mindedness scale: factor structure, convergent validity and gender in a non-psychiatric sample. *Psychology & Psychotherapy: Theory, Research and Practice*, *75*: 131–150.

Shonfeld-Ringel, S. (2001). The effect of culture on the working alliance between Asian American clients and Western therapists. *Dissertation Abstracts International*, *61*(11-A).

Sifneos, P. E. (1979). *Short-term Psychotherapy: Evaluation and Technique*. New York: Plenum Press.

Smith, R. (2001). Why doctors are so unhappy? *British Medical Journal*, *322*: §073–1074.

Snowden, P., & Kane, E. (2003). Personality disorder: no longer a diagnosis of exclusion. (Editorial.) *Psychiatric Bulletin*, *27*: 401–403.

Sotsky, S. M., Glass, D., Shea, M., Pilkonis, P., Collins, P., Elkin, J., Watkins, J., Iruber, S., Leber, W., Moyer, J., & Oliveri, M. (1991). Patients' predictors of response to psychotherapy and pharmacotherapy: finding in the NIMH treatment of depression collaborative research programme. *American Journal of Psychiatry*, *148*: 997–1008.

Soutter, A., & Garelick, A. (1999). What is the role of pre-assessment questionnaires in psychotherapy? *Psychoanalytical Psychotherapy*, *13*: 245–258.

Spurling, L. (2003). On the therapeutic value of not offering psychotherapy: an account of an extended assessment. *Psychoanalytical Psychotherapy, 17*(1): 1–17.

Stern, D. N. (1985). *The Interpersonal World of the Infant.* New York: Basic Books.

Szasz, T. S. (1970). *The Manufacture of Madness.* New York: Dell.

Target, M., & Fonagy, P. (1994). The efficacy of psychoanalysis for children with emotional disorders. *Journal of the American Academy of Child & Adolescent Psychiatry, 33*: 361–371.

Thomä, H., & Kächele, H. (1987). *Psychoanalytic Practice, Volume 1: Principles.* Trans. M. Wilson & D. Roseveare. New York: Springer-Verlag.

Truant, G. S. (1998). Assessment of suitability for psychotherapy. I. Introduction and the assessment process. *American Journal of Psychotherapy, 52*(4): 397–411.

Truant, G. S. (1999). Assessment of suitability for psychotherapy. II. Assessment based on basic process goals. *American Journal of Psychotherapy, 53*(1): 17–33.

Turner, R. M. (1987). The effect of personality disorder diagnosis on the outcome of social anxiety symptom reduction. *Journal of Personality Disorders, 1*: 136–143.

Tyson, P., & Tyson, R. L. (1990). *Psychoanalytic Theories of Development: An Integration.* New Haven: Yale University Press.

Tyson, R., & Sandler, J. (1971). Problems in the selection of patients for psychoanalysis: comments on the application of the concept of "indications", "suitability" and "analysabilty". *British Journal of Medical Psychology, 44*: 211–228.

Wallerstein, R. (1965). The goals of psychoanalysis: survey of analytic viewpoints. *Journal of the American Psychoanalytical Association, 13*: 748–770.

Wallerstein, R. (1986). *Forty-two Lives in Treatment. A Study of Psychoanalysis and Psychotherapy.* New York: Guildford Press.

Weber, J., Bachrach, H., & Solomon, M. (1985). Factors associated with the outcome of psychoanalysis: Report of the Columbia Psychoanalytic Centre Research Project II. *International Review of Psychoanalysis, 12*: 127–141.

Webster, A. (1992). The effect of pre-assessment information on clients' satisfaction, expectations and attendance at a mental day centre. *British Journal of Medical Psychology, 65*: 89–93.

Weinryb, R., & Rossel, R. (1991). Karolinska psychodynamic profile. *Acta. Psychiat. Scand. Supp., 363*: 83.

Wilczek, A., Weinryb R., Gustavsson, P., Barber, J., Schubert, J., & Asperg, M. (1998). Symptoms and character traits in patients selected for long-term psychodynamic psychotherapy. *Journal of Psychotherapy Practice & Research, 7*(1): 23–34.

Wilson, M. (1993). *DSM III* and the transformation of American psychiatry. *American Journal of Psychiatry, 150*: 399–410.

Wright, J. H., & Davis, D. (1994). The therapeutic relationship in cognitive-behavioural therapy. Patient perceptions and therapist responses. *Cognitive and Behavioural Practice, 1*(1): 25–45.

Yalom, I. D. (1995). *The Theory and Practice of Group Psychotherapy* (4th edn). New York: Basic Books.

INDEX

O'Brien, C., 58, 88
object relationships, 50, 52–54, 56, 58, 63
obsessive behaviour, 25, 55
Ogrodniczuk, J., 49, 88
Olinick, S. L., 59, 90
Oliveri, M., 43, 92
Olmsted, M. P., 42, 85
Orlinsky, D. E., xvi, 59, 90
Padilla-Cotto, L., 48, 83
Paolitto, F., 71, 87
Pappanastassiou, M., 36, 86
Parks, B., 59, 90
Parry, G., 3, 5, 71, 90
Partridge, E., 7, 90
patient choice, 2
Patients' Charter, 2
patient–doctor relationship(s), 2, 4
Pazzagli, A., 34, 37, 90
pensée opératoire, 54
Perez-Prado, E. M., 48, 83
Perry, C., 63, 88
Perry, S., 23, 61, 90
personality disorders, 25–26, 33–35, 52, 54, 57 see also: classification systems
pharmacological/drug therapy, 14, 22, 24, 62
Picard, S., 57, 84
Pilkonis, P., 43, 53, 89, 92
Pine, F., 53, 90
Piper, W. E., 47, 49, 53, 56, 88, 90
Plutchik, R., 57, 84
post-assessment routes/options, 69
Priebe, S., 19, 88
Proietti, J., 53, 89
psychodynamic formulation, 62
psychological mindedness, 47–49, 59–60
psychotherapeutic contact, 25
psychotherapist(s), 23, 37, 52, 60, 64
psychotherapy/psychotherapies, 3, 8, 13–14, 18–20, 22–25, 37, 43–44, 46, 48, 51, 53, 56, 60, 70–71

assessment, 4–5, 7–11, 14–29, 32–38, 40–47, 49, 52–55, 58–59, 61–62, 64–65, 69–71, 73–74
    consultation, 8, 13, 27, 36
    forensic units, 37
    group, 43, 71
    in-depth, 54
    journey/process and outcome, 12, 58
    out-patient, 57
    pre-assessment questionnaire, 17
    prescription, 8
    psychoanalytic, 43
    psychodynamic, 19, 24, 27, 39, 45–46, 49–50, 56, 60, 62–63, 66, 70, 74
    referral, 13, 23, 25–26, 64
    research, 33
    services, 71
    short-term, 49
    Type A (integral), 4, 16
    Type B (generic), 4, 16
    Type C (formal), 4
    types/modalities, 4, 15–16, 23, 28, 44, 60–62, 67, 69–72, 74
quality control, 2
questionnaire, see: assessment

Ratho, R., 49, 84
Rees, A., 34, 92
referral(s), 16, 18–19, 21–22, 26, 35, 40–41, 70
    criteria, 19
    letter, 14–15, 19, 21, 26, 28–29, 61–62, 64, 76
    mode of, 19
    pre-referral stage, 13, 73
    process of, 5, 13–20, 69
    reasons for, 14–15, 18
    route, 15–16
    source, 14
relationship to reality (reality testing), 50–52, 56 see also: adaptation to reality